START

Building Confidence, Creating Happiness, and Overcoming Anxiety and Depression

Hans Watson, DO

University Elite Press

Paperback ISBN: 978-1-972981-03-0
Hardcover ISBN: 978-1-972981-04-7
eBook ISBN: 978-1-972981-05-4

This book is intended for educational purposes only and is not a substitute for professional medical or mental health advice, diagnosis, or treatment.

First Edition

Contents

Introduction 5

Chapter 1: The Pattern 8

Chapter 2: How Change Actually Begins 13

Chapter 3: Living in the Up Arrow and Down Arrow 26

Chapter 4: What Avoidance Actually Looks Like 33

Chapter 5: Not All Stepping Away Is Avoidance 42

Chapter 6: Where to Start 49

Chapter 7: Building Momentum 53

Chapter 8: When You Get Stuck 57

Chapter 9: Your Past Still Influences You 61

Chapter 10: Your Future Begins Now 66

References 70

INTRODUCTION

Alex first came to see me with crippling anxiety, overwhelming depression, and thoughts of suicide. He was twenty years old, but in many ways he was functioning closer to someone much younger. He sat quietly while his grandmother did most of the talking, explaining his situation in a way that sounded both concerned and resigned. She had driven him to the appointment, checked him in, and began describing his struggles as if they were something that had simply happened to him. She explained that he had anxiety and depression, that he had always struggled, and that he seemed to be one of the unfortunate ones who just ended up this way. As she spoke, it was clear that both of them saw his situation as something outside of their control, something that had occurred almost by coincidence, without any meaningful influence from behavior or environment.

The dynamic in the room was just as revealing as the words being used. This was not a conversation between a clinician and an independent adult seeking help. It was closer to what you might expect if a child had been brought in by a caregiver who was used to managing everything for them. When Alex was asked a question, his grandmother would often answer for him or step in to clarify what he "meant." When something difficult came up, she would soften it or redirect it. Her intention was to protect him, but that pattern had been in place for a long time.

Alex's history reflected that pattern. His parents had him at a young age and eventually chose not to take responsibility for raising him, leaving him in the care of his grandmother. She stepped in and provided stability, but she also struggled to tolerate seeing him uncomfortable, frustrated, or overwhelmed. Whenever he encountered something difficult, she intervened. Whenever he struggled, she made things easier. Over time, without realizing it, she removed many of the experiences that would have required him to grow.

By the time he reached adulthood, life had begun to demand things from him that he had never been required to learn. He did not know how to function socially, did not know how to persist through difficulty, and had not developed the ability to take responsibility for himself. When those expectations showed up, his response was not to engage with them, but to avoid them, because avoidance was the only pattern he had consistently practiced. As those patterns continued, his anxiety increased to the point that even simple interactions felt overwhelming, his confidence steadily decreased, and the world around him began to feel more and more unmanageable. Over time, his depression deepened alongside that narrowing of his life, and there were periods where things became serious enough that he experienced thoughts of not wanting to continue living, not as a constant state, but enough to recognize how far things had progressed.

When we began working together, I asked him what he wanted his life to look like. He struggled to answer, and the only clear response he could give was that he wanted less anxiety and less depression. That answer led us into a deeper discussion about what life without anxiety and depression would actually require. When we shifted the conversation toward goals, his answers became clearer, but also more revealing.

He said he wanted to play more guitar, spend more time on video games, and do more of the things he already enjoyed. From his perspective, these were positive goals. In reality, they required no meaningful change. They did not force him to engage with any of the areas of his life that were contributing to his struggles. They allowed him to stay exactly where he was while feeling like he was doing something to improve.

Over time, this pattern had a predictable effect. The more Alex avoided what was difficult, the more his grandmother stepped in to try to help him, and the less capable he became. The less capable he felt, the more overwhelming life became, and the more overwhelming life became, the more both of them leaned into the same pattern of avoidance and protection. What they were experiencing was not random, and it was not simply the result of bad luck. It was a reinforcing cycle that was steadily moving him in a specific direction, one that led to worsening depression, increasing anxiety, decreasing independence, a growing inability to function in the real world and thoughts of suicide.

What makes Alex's story important is that it is not unique. Most people will not see themselves in his exact situation, but they will recognize parts of his pattern in their own life. People struggling with anxiety, depression or suicidal thought will often see that they avoid difficult conversations, delay important decisions, or stay in areas where they feel comfortable instead of engaging with what actually needs to change. They may call it being busy, being careful, or waiting for the right time, but the direction is often the same. Over time, their world becomes smaller, their confidence decreases, and the problems they were trying to avoid become more difficult to manage.

For some readers, this way of understanding these patterns will build directly on ideas introduced elsewhere, particularly the recognition that certain patterns in life consistently pull people toward anxiety, depression, and isolation. For others, this may be the first time the ideas are being considered in a structured way. Regardless of where you are starting, the focus here is the same. The goal is not simply to recognize how these patterns are connected to mental struggles, but to understand what it takes to begin moving in a different direction and to build the capacity required to change them over time.

Experiences like anxiety, depression, and even suicidal thinking do not develop randomly. They follow a pattern.[14, 15, 30] Conversely, experiences like happiness, resilience and success do not develop randomly either. They also follow a pattern.[10, 17, 23] While the details of each person's life are different, the underlying processes that move someone toward or away from those outcomes are remarkably consistent.

In this book, I will refer to the pattern as the Adversity Cycle. Every time you face something difficult, you respond to it. When you move toward it, you build the ability to handle it. When you move away from it, the problem grows. What feels easier in the moment often creates greater difficulty over time, while what feels more difficult in the moment is often what leads to long-term improvement.

If that pattern continues long enough, the consequences compound. It is rarely a single decision that creates a problem. It is the accumulation of small decisions to avoid what is difficult, repeated across different areas of life, until confidence decreases, opportunities narrow, and the future begins to feel limited. In many cases, this is the path through which anxiety increases, depression develops, and in its most severe form, hopelessness can progress to suicidal thinking.

At the same time, the opposite pattern is also true. When people begin to engage with what they have been avoiding, even in small ways, something starts to change. They begin to build capacity. Situations that once felt overwhelming start to feel more manageable. Confidence begins to increase, not because life has become easier, but because they have become more capable.

Research consistently shows that two of the most powerful modifiable factors influencing mental health are healthy social connection[17] and meaningful accomplishment,[10] and both require engagement with life rather than avoidance.

Through working with and supervising the care of thousands of patients, I have consistently seen this same pattern determine whether someone remains stuck or begins to improve. When people continue to avoid what is difficult, their world tends to shrink. When they begin to engage with it, even in small ways, things begin to change.

Alex's anxiety and depression did not improve because his life suddenly had fewer challenges, or because he was one of the lucky ones. They improved when he began to do something he had never consistently done before. He began to face what he had been avoiding, and in doing so, he started to build the skills that had been missing for most of his life, which ultimately allowed him to function more effectively in the real world and move his life in a different direction, and that process, learning how to engage with what is difficult in a way that builds capacity over time, is the foundation of what this book is designed to teach.

CHAPTER 1

The Pattern

When Alex began to make small changes in his life, the results did not appear dramatic at first. There was no sudden transformation, no moment where everything became easy or where his disabling anxiety, severe depression, or thoughts of suicide disappeared overnight. What changed was something much more subtle, but also much more important. The direction of his behavior began to shift.

At the beginning, most of his decisions followed a predictable pattern. When something felt uncomfortable, uncertain, or overwhelming, his instinct was to move away from it. This showed up in simple ways. He avoided conversations that felt awkward, delayed decisions that felt stressful, and retreated into activities that allowed him to feel some level of comfort without requiring him to engage with the parts of life that were challenging. In the moment, those decisions felt reasonable. They reduced discomfort, gave him relief, and allowed him to regain a sense of control. However, over time, those same decisions began to create a very different outcome.

Each time he avoided something difficult, he missed an opportunity to learn how to handle it. Each missed opportunity made the next situation feel more overwhelming, not less. As those experiences accumulated, his confidence did not simply remain low—it diminished in the areas he consistently avoided, and that loss of confidence made even simple situations feel increasingly unmanageable. This is often how anxiety begins to increase, not as something random, but as a response to repeatedly feeling unable to handle what life requires.

This pattern did not stay isolated to a single part of his life. It began to spread. The more situations he avoided, the fewer areas of life he felt capable in. As his sense of capability decreased, his willingness to engage decreased as well. Over time, his world became smaller, his options became more limited, and the future began to feel less open and more constrained. What had once been a manageable level of discomfort began to feel overwhelming, and that sense of overwhelm fed directly into his anxiety and discouragement.

As this continued, the emotional impact deepened. The repeated experience of avoiding, feeling incapable, and facing growing difficulty led to a level of discouragement that is common in people who struggle with depression. It was not the result of a single event, but the accumulation of many small moments where he moved away from what was difficult. Over time, those moments built into a pattern that made progress feel less likely and the future feel less hopeful. In more severe cases, when this pattern continues long enough without interruption and across multiple areas of life, that sense of hopelessness can deepen into thoughts of not wanting to continue at all.

At the time, neither Alex nor his grandmother saw this pattern clearly. From their perspective, his anxiety, depression, and thoughts of suicide were simply conditions he had developed, something that had happened to him rather than something that had been shaped over time. Because they saw it that way, their attempts to solve the problem focused solely on reducing the symptoms rather than addressing the underlying pattern that caused the depression and anxiety. They tried to make things easier, reduce stress, and avoid situations that made him uncomfortable. While those efforts were well-intentioned, by avoiding adversity, they reinforced the very pattern that was creating the problem.

The type of adversity that leads to growth does not appear randomly or by coincidence. It is the result of pursuing something that matters.[10] When you have goals, you will inevitably encounter challenges. Those challenges create a decision point. You can move toward them and attempt to work through them, or you can move away from them and seek relief. That decision, repeated over time, ultimately determines the direction of your life.

If a person consistently moves toward those challenges, they begin to build the ability to handle them. That ability becomes confidence, and as confidence builds across different areas of life, it contributes to a sense of self-esteem that is grounded in experience. This is not something that appears suddenly or without cause. It is built through repeated experiences of engaging with difficulty across multiple areas of life and learning that you can handle it.

If a person consistently moves away from those challenges, the opposite occurs. Problems do not disappear. They accumulate. As they accumulate, they create more pressure, more stress, and more situations that feel overwhelming. The person's confidence decreases because they have fewer experiences of successfully handling difficulty, and as that confidence decreases, self-esteem begins to erode and anxiety increases. Over time, this leads to the discouragement and low mood that are commonly experienced as depression, and when this pattern persists across multiple areas of life, the emotional impact can become severe.

This pattern is what we will refer to as the Adversity Cycle. It is not a theory based on abstract ideas. It is a practical framework that describes how people respond to the challenges in their life and how those responses shape their outcomes over time. Every person encounters adversity. What differs is how they respond to it, and that response determines whether they build the capacity to move forward or become increasingly limited by the situations they face. (My patients have found it improves their capabilities to see it if they take the time to repeatedly write the diagram of the adversity cycle until they learn it by heart.)

In Alex's case, this cycle had been operating for years without being clearly identified. Once it became visible, it created a different set of options. Instead of continuing to move away from difficulty, he began to experiment with moving toward it, even in small ways. Those early attempts were not perfect, and they were often uncomfortable, but they marked the beginning of a shift. He was no longer reinforcing the same pattern that had created the anxiety and depression. He was beginning to build something new.

That shift did not immediately eliminate all his anxiety, depression, or thoughts of suicide, but it changed the trajectory. Instead of moving further into a pattern that increased those experiences, he began to move in a direction that gradually reduced them. That change in direction is the foundation of everything that follows, because it shows that these patterns are not fixed. They can be recognized, understood, and changed over time through consistent engagement with what is difficult.

As you will see, Alex started to engage with what he had been avoiding, even in small ways, and the pattern that had defined his life began to shift. It did not happen quickly, and it did not happen all at once, but as he began to face what was in front of him, he started to build the skills he had been missing. Over time, that engagement led to increased confidence, and that confidence made it possible for him to take on challenges that had once felt overwhelming.

This is the same pattern that applies to everyone. The details of your adversity may be different, but the underlying process remains consistent. When you move toward what is difficult, you build your ability to handle it. When you move away from it, you reduce that ability. The more consistently you do one or the other, the more your experience begins to reflect that direction. Understanding this does not make the process easy, but it does make it clear, and that clarity is what allows you to begin making different choices that, over time, change the direction of your life.

Chapter 1 Summary

- Life is not random; there are patterns that determine whether things get better or worse.
- The Adversity Cycle explains how your response to difficulty shapes your outcomes over time.
- Moving toward adversity (up arrow) builds capacity, confidence, and progress.
- Moving away from adversity (down arrow) creates temporary relief but allows problems to build over time.
- Confidence is built through repeated engagement with challenges across different areas of life.
- The difference between feeling capable and feeling stuck is often how consistently you choose to engage or avoid.

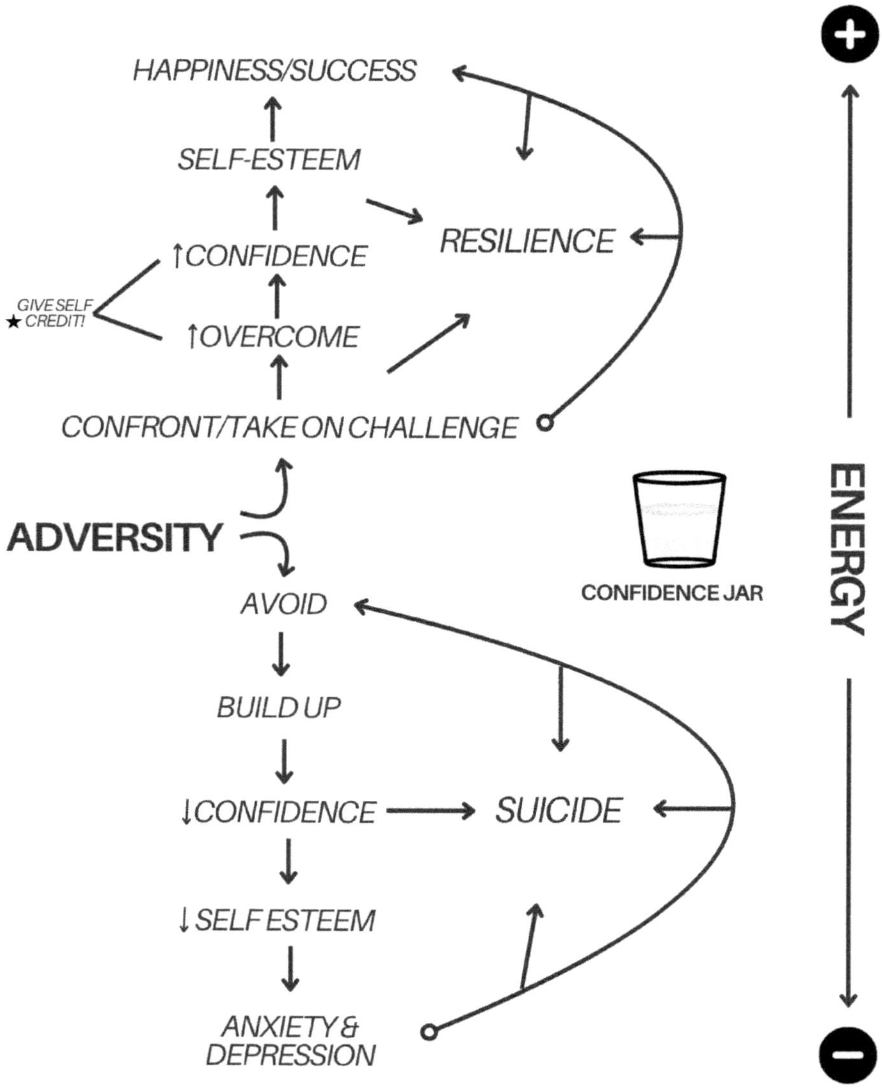
HAPPINESS/SUCCESS
SELF-ESTEEM
↑CONFIDENCE
RESILIENCE
GIVE SELF CREDIT!
↑OVERCOME
CONFRONT/TAKE ON CHALLENGE
ADVERSITY
AVOID
CONFIDENCE JAR
ENERGY
BUILD UP
↓CONFIDENCE
SUICIDE
↓SELF ESTEEM
ANXIETY & DEPRESSION

CHAPTER 2

How Change Actually Begins

I remember being in a group one time where someone was talking about a mutual friend of ours and made the comment that he was just lucky to have been born confident. Several people in the group agreed, and the conversation moved on as if that explained everything. What they didn't understand was that this person had experienced more adversity than most of them could imagine. As a teenager, he went through his parents' divorce and was forced to move from a place where he felt comfortable into a completely different environment. By the time he was in middle and high school, he was largely supporting himself. He had to work to earn money, often buying his own food, finding clothes at thrift stores, and figuring out how to survive without the level of support most people take for granted.

Over time, he continued to take on more responsibility, more challenges, and more uncertainty. He didn't become confident because he was born that way. He became confident because he repeatedly faced situations that required him to grow, adapt, and push through things that would have caused most people to withdraw. Eventually, that process increased his confidence and led him to opportunities that were once considered out of reach, including playing professional football and later building a successful career and life beyond it. People who only saw the end result assumed confidence had always been there, but in reality, it had been built step by step through years of confronting adversity.

That same principle is what began to change things for Alex, although it did not look nearly as dramatic in the beginning. His progress did not start with a major breakthrough or a sudden shift in how he saw himself. It started much smaller, in ways that were easy to overlook but incredibly important over time. When he first came to therapy, he did not want to be there, and most of the early sessions were spent with him focusing on what other people were doing wrong rather than looking at himself. When the focus shifted toward his own behavior, his instinct was to deflect, to joke, or to redirect the conversation away from anything uncomfortable. At times he would even dissociate into a dreamlike state when conversations became emotionally difficult, but despite all of that, he continued to show up and stay engaged even when those moments were uncomfortable.

At the time, that may not have seemed like progress, but it was one of the first times he consistently chose to do something he would normally avoid. Each time he showed up, even when he did not feel like it, he was engaging with something that was uncomfortable for him. Each time he stayed in a conversation that focused on his own behavior instead of escaping it, he was doing something different than he had done before. Those moments were small, and they did not immediately change how he felt about himself, but they created movement where there had previously been none.

This is one of the most common misunderstandings about change. People assume that confidence, motivation, and the ability to handle life's challenges are things you either have or you do not have. They believe that once they understand their situation well enough, something will suddenly shift, or they assume that anxiety, depression, and even suicidal thinking are simply things that happen to certain people who are unlucky or predisposed to them. While biological and genetic factors can influence how people experience these challenges, that explanation alone is incomplete.[1, 10, 24, 31-34, 41]

If these conditions were entirely fixed or predetermined, changes in behavior would not consistently lead to improvement. Yet both clinical experience and research show that when people begin to engage differently with their lives, symptoms often improve. That tells us something important. It tells us that while biology may influence the starting point, behavior plays a significant role in determining the direction things move over time.

Understanding is important, and it is often the first step, but understanding alone does not create change. It has to be combined with intention and, most importantly, with action. Real change begins when your behavior starts to move in a different direction in a way that is observable and measurable. It is not enough to think differently about your situation or to want things to improve. There has to be real progress, even if it is small. That progress is what starts to shift how you experience your life and begins to change the pattern that has been keeping you stuck.

This is one of the reasons anxiety, depression, hopelessness, and reduced self-esteem often persist for so long. Many people spend years trying to feel differently by simply thinking differently and avoid behaving differently. They wait to feel motivated before taking action, wait to feel confident before engaging with adversity, or wait to feel emotionally ready before pursuing meaningful change. In reality, those feelings usually begin to change only after behavior changes first. Action comes before confidence, not after it.

What began changing Alex's life was not that he suddenly became fearless, motivated, or emotionally healthy. It was that he began engaging with what he would normally avoid, even in small ways, and that engagement slowly started creating evidence that he was capable of more than he believed. Over time, those experiences accumulated, and the direction of his life began to shift because his behavior had begun to shift first.

How Confidence Is Built

To understand how real change happens over time, it helps to look more closely at what is actually being built when you begin to engage with your life differently. Earlier, we talked about how progress begins when your behavior changes in a measurable way. What that progress creates, step by step, is confidence.

One of the most useful ways to understand this process is to recognize that confidence is not something you either have or do not have. It is something that develops over time through repeated experiences. Each time you confront something difficult and make progress, even in a small way, you prove that you are capable of handling more than you thought. That evidence does not always feel significant in the moment, and it often does not stand out as a major breakthrough, but it is real, and it accumulates.

A helpful way to visualize this is to think of your confidence like a jar that slowly fills over time, one drop at a time. Each time you move toward something difficult and engage with it, you add a drop of confidence oil to that jar. Early on, those drops may seem almost insignificant. You may look at your situation and feel like very little has changed, but the process has already begun. Those small actions are building something that was not there before.

Even when you do not succeed on the first attempt, you are still adding to that jar. When you struggle, adjust, and try again, you are learning and adapting, and that adaptation creates additional drops. In many cases, the process of failing, learning, and continuing forward adds more to your confidence than immediate success would have, because it teaches you that you can recover, adjust, and keep going. Over time, those drops begin to accumulate, and what once felt empty starts to fill.

The opposite pattern is just as important to understand. When you consistently move away from what is in front of you, you are not simply staying in the same place. You are reinforcing the belief that you cannot handle what is in front of you. Over time, that belief becomes stronger, and in that sense, avoidance does not just pause progress. It actively reduces confidence. It is as if you are removing drops of oil from your jar, gradually lowering the amount of evidence you have that you are capable of handling your life.

This is why confidence does not come before action. It comes from action. People often believe they need to feel confident before they take on something difficult, but that expectation works against them. Confidence is built by engaging with adversity, not by waiting for a feeling that has not yet been earned. Each time you take action and follow through, even in a small way, you are adding to your capacity, and that capacity is what eventually becomes confidence.

This is exactly what was beginning to happen for Alex, even before he recognized it. Each time he showed up to therapy, each time he stayed in a conversation that made him uncomfortable, and each time he chose not to avoid what was in front of him, he was adding drops to that jar. At the time, those moments did not feel like major accomplishments, but over time they began to change how he experienced himself and what he believed he was capable of handling.

One of the mistakes people often make is assuming that confidence automatically creates self-esteem, but confidence and self-esteem are not exactly the same thing. Confidence tends to build within specific areas of your life. You can become more capable and confident in one area while still feeling uncertain or avoidant in another. This is why it is possible for someone to be highly successful professionally while struggling deeply in their personal life. You can see people who have built enormous confidence in their career while simultaneously struggling with anxiety, depression and suicidal thinking that are fed by social isolation or romantic disconnection.

When certain areas are consistently avoided, confidence in those areas does not develop, and that gap often becomes a source of anxiety, limitation, and reduced self-esteem. Over time, self-esteem is shaped not simply by success in one area, but by how consistently you engage across the major areas of your life. This is one of the reasons people can appear successful externally while internally feeling deeply inadequate, depressed, anxious and suicidal. They may have built confidence in one domain but neglecting others still creates anxiety, shame, instability, or discouragement in other domains.

As you continue to add drops of confidence in one area, your capacity in that area grows, but that does not automatically transfer to every other part of your life. Over time, the goal is not just to build confidence in one place, but to expand it across multiple areas to build a full and rich life. As that happens, your overall sense of capability and stability begins to change in a more complete way.

Another way to think about this is that your confidence jar does not stay the same size forever. As you grow, mature and take on more responsibility, what is required of you increases, but the confidence jar expands. Early on, even a few drops can feel meaningful. Over time, as your life becomes more complex and your goals become larger, it takes more and more engagement to maintain that same sense of confidence. This is why the process does not stop. You are always either adding to that reservoir or taking away from it based on how you respond to what is in front of you.

As this process continues, something begins to shift internally. You start to feel more capable in a wider range of circumstances. Situations that once felt overwhelming now feel more manageable. The sense of being stuck loosens, not because everything has been solved, but because you are no longer standing still. That movement is what builds confidence over time, and it becomes something you can rely on as you continue to face new challenges and move toward your true potential.

Visions and Goals

This is exactly where Alex initially struggled when he first began therapy. His focus was on reducing anxiety and avoiding discomfort, and when he was asked what he wanted his life to look like, his answers stayed within what was already familiar to him. He wanted to spend more time doing things he already enjoyed and avoid situations that made him uncomfortable. From his perspective, those felt like reasonable goals, but they did not lead him to facing the adversity that would improve his situation.

The type of adversity that leads to growth does not appear randomly or by coincidence. It is the result of pursuing something that matters. When you have goals, you will inevitably encounter challenges. Those challenges create a decision point. You can move toward them and attempt to work through them, or you can move away from them and seek temporary relief. That decision, repeated over time, determines the direction of your life.

In many cases, the most important adversity is not something you choose. It is something that is already present in your life that you would prefer to avoid, minimize, or ignore, but that still requires engagement if things are going to improve. This is why meaningful growth often begins when a person stops organizing their life around temporary comfort and begins organizing it around a vision of what they want their life to become.

This is where it becomes necessary to clarify something that is often overlooked. Meaningful goals do not exist in isolation. They come from a clear vision of what success would look like. Before someone can identify the right goals, they have to answer a more fundamental question, which is what kind of life they are trying to build and what kind of person they want to become. In my work, this is often one of the most challenging parts of the process. Many people have never clearly defined what success actually looks like for them, and as a result, they struggle to create goals that move them in a meaningful direction.

A meaningful vision of success is not vague or limited to one area of life. It involves a clear understanding of what a successful life looks like across multiple areas, including professional development, romantic relationships, family relationships, social life and hobbies, and spiritual or ethical values. Without this clarity, it becomes difficult to set goals that lead to meaningful progress, because there is no defined direction to move toward.

This matters for another reason as well. Human beings consistently require two things in order to thrive psychologically: healthy social connection and meaningful accomplishment. Healthy social connection is more than simply being around people. At its core, it involves feeling heard, seen, and appreciated by others. When those needs are consistently unmet, people tend to feel increasingly isolated, discouraged, and disconnected, even if they are surrounded by other people.

At the same time, healthy social connection by itself is usually not enough to create lasting stability or fulfillment. People also need a sense of meaningful accomplishment, which comes from engaging with life in a way that builds capability, contribution, and progress over time. This is where vision becomes essential. Without a clear vision of success across the major areas of life, it becomes difficult to consistently pursue the kinds of goals that produce meaningful accomplishment.

When this vision has not been developed, people often default toward whatever provides the fastest or easiest experience of being heard, seen, and appreciated. In many cases, this leads to an overreliance on the social and hobbies area of life, because it provides immediate connection, stimulation, novelty, and relief without requiring the same level of sustained responsibility or growth found in the other areas. The problem is not that social connection or hobbies are unhealthy. The problem is that they don't function well, as a long term substitute, for growth in other areas of your life that are being avoided.

Over time, this creates an imbalance that becomes increasingly important. Responsibilities related to professional development, relationships, family, discipline, or ethical growth are neglected and begin to feel overwhelming or excessive because they are not connected to a larger vision of success. Instead of being understood as meaningful parts of building a stable and fulfilling life, the responsibilities in these life areas are experienced as unrelated chores that interfere with comfort and immediate gratification that come with social or play activities.

This is one of the reasons some people feel overwhelmed by basic adult responsibilities while others are able to engage with those same responsibilities more naturally. The difference is often not the number of tasks, but whether those tasks are connected to a meaningful vision that makes them feel purposeful in all life areas. Without that framework, responsibilities feel endless, disconnected, and draining. With it, they become part of building the kind of life and relationships a person actually wants.

This dynamic becomes particularly important in relationships. If one partner is actively pursuing growth across multiple life areas, they often feel heard, seen, and appreciated through shared effort, contribution, reliability, and accomplishment in various life areas and settings. If the other partner continues seeking to fulfill those same needs primarily through novelty, entertainment, or social stimulation, that partner tends to miss growth-producing responsibilities and their lack of maturation becomes difficult to ignore. Over time, this can create tension, resentment, and a growing sense that the two individuals are moving in fundamentally different directions.

This does not mean that the partner in the developmentally arrested position is incapable of growth. In many cases, it simply means that a clear vision of success has not yet been fully developed. Once that vision begins to form, goals become more meaningful, engagement becomes more consistent, maturation continues and the responsibilities that once felt overwhelming begin to feel reasonable.

Once the focus shifted toward defining what success would actually look like for Alex, the difficulty of his daily life initially increased. Real goals required him to acknowledge the areas where he was struggling and accept that moving forward would involve doing things that felt uncomfortable, unfamiliar, and at times overwhelming. The increased difficulty was not a sign that something was wrong. It was a sign that he was beginning to look at something that actually mattered.

When you define a meaningful vision for your life, goals begin to take on a different role. They are no longer just things you would like to accomplish. They become the steps required to move toward healing from anxiety, overcoming depression and becoming the person you are capable of becoming. Each of those steps introduces a form of adversity, because moving toward something meaningful will always require effort, adjustment, and a willingness to engage with difficulty.

This is why I often describe meaningful goals as "dragons." A real goal is something that, when you look at it honestly, creates resistance. It is something that requires you to stretch beyond what is currently comfortable and engage with parts of your life that you would otherwise avoid. That resistance is not something to be eliminated. It is something to be recognized, because it is often an indicator that you are moving toward something that has real value.

Every dragon is guarding something valuable. In this case, it is guarding what you might think of as a pot of gold. That pot of gold represents the growth, capability, and confidence that comes from working through the challenge in front of you. It is not something that can be obtained without effort, it is not something that can be reached by staying within what is already comfortable and it will always result in a few battle scars.

As you begin to fight your dragons, even imperfectly, you gain something in return. Each attempt, each adjustment, and each step forward adds to your experience and builds your capacity. In terms of the confidence jar we discussed earlier, each of those moments adds drops of confidence oil. When you struggle, adapt, and try again, you are not falling behind. As long as you learn from your struggles and failures, you are gaining additional drops that would not exist without that process. In many cases, the learning and adjustment that come from difficulty add more to your confidence than immediate success would have, because they teach you how to recover, think differently, and continue forward.

At the same time, it is important to recognize that not all goals are truly an example of facing adversity. Some goals allow you to stay comfortable while giving you a false sense of being productive. They often involve doing more of what you already enjoy or what you are already good at, and while they may create a sense of movement, they do not require meaningful change. These types of goals can feel satisfying in the moment, but they do not create the kind of adversity that leads to growth and the ability to overcome depression, anxiety or suicidal thoughts.

This distinction becomes important because it is one of the ways people unintentionally maintain the patterns that keep them stuck. When goals do not require you to engage with what is difficult, they allow you to avoid the very areas of your life that need to improve. As a result, the process that builds confidence, increases self-esteem, and reduces anxiety and depression does not fully activate.

What is required instead is a different kind of goal, one that is tied to a meaningful vision and that creates enough resistance to force growth. These goals are not comfortable, and they are not supposed to be. They are designed to push you into the areas where growth is needed.

That does not mean you have to take on everything at once. Trying to confront every challenge in your life simultaneously is one of the fastest ways to become overwhelmed and retreat back into avoidance. Instead, the process begins by identifying where meaningful progress is needed and starting to engage with it in a way that is manageable. Over time, this expands into other life areas, but it does not begin with every life area all at once.

When you look at it this way, it becomes easier to understand why so many people feel stuck. It is not just that they are randomly struggling with anxiety, depression or suicidal thoughts. It is that they often don't have a clearly defined vision of success, and without that, they do not have meaningful goals that create the kind of adversity required for anxiety and depression defeating growth. Without meaningful adversity, there is nothing to engage with, and the process that builds confidence and reduces symptoms never fully activates.

This is where everything begins to come together. At this point you have seen the pattern that explains why things feel the way they do. You understand that change requires real, measurable ways of confronting adversity. You see how confidence is only built through repeated engagement with adversity, which means you can begin to attack it intentionally rather than waiting for it to overwhelm you.

Organizing Your Life Into Five Areas

If you understand where adversity comes from and how progress begins, the next challenge is figuring out how to apply that in a way that does not feel overwhelming. One of the most common reactions people have at this point is recognizing that there are multiple areas of life that need attention, and the idea of trying to address all of them at once can feel discouraging. Without a clear structure, people often either try to do too much and burn out or avoid the process altogether because it feels too large to manage.

To make this process more manageable, it helps to break life down into a small number of clearly defined areas. Instead of trying to fix everything at once, you can begin to identify where you are making progress, where you are avoiding, and where engagement is needed. Over time, this allows you to move forward in a structured way without losing sight of the bigger picture.

In my work, I have found that most of what people struggle with can be organized into five primary areas of life. These areas provide a simple but effective framework for understanding where growth is needed and where confidence is being built or lost.

The Five Life Areas

Professional life

Romantic Relationships

Family Relationships

Social Life & Hobbies

Spiritual & Ethical Development.

Each of these areas represents a different part of your life where goals can be set, adversity can be encountered, and progress can be made. When you look at your life through this lens, it becomes easier to identify where you are consistently moving in an upward direction and where you may be avoiding something that needs to be addressed. It also helps explain why someone can feel confident and capable in one area while feeling completely stuck in another, because each area has its own set of challenges and requires its own engagement.

Over time, your overall sense of confidence and self-esteem is shaped by how consistently you engage across these areas rather than by success in any single one. This is one of the reasons people can become highly developed in one area of life while still struggling significantly in others. As a reminder, we often see a person build confidence professionally while still struggling with depression because they are emotionally disconnected, socially isolated or spiritually aimless. Regardless of how successful the person appears in one life area, consistently avoiding other life areas predictably erodes self-esteem and creates anxiety, depression, suicidal thinking, instability and discouragement.

Another important aspect of this framework is that these areas are not completely separate from one another. In reality, they overlap. Progress in one area will often carry over into others. For example, improving your ability to communicate socially will also improve your ability to communicate and interact with your family and romantic relationships. In many cases it will influence how you function professionally as well. In terms of the confidence jar, this means that even when you are focused on adding drops of confidence oil in one area, some of those gains naturally benefit multiple areas. This is encouraging, because it means progress is often more powerful than it first appears.

At the same time, this overlap does not eliminate the need to eventually engage with each area directly. If certain areas are consistently avoided, they will continue to create friction, anxiety, limitation, and reduced confidence over time regardless of how much progress is made elsewhere. This is one of the reasons people sometimes feel confused about why they still struggle emotionally even when one part of their life appears to be going well. Growth in one area helps, but it does not fully compensate for directly engaging in another.

That does not mean you need to take on everything at once. In fact, trying to do that would likely be overwhelming and counterproductive. Different phases of life naturally require different levels of attention in each area. There will be times where more of your energy is focused on professional development with the remainder being spread on the other life areas. Other times you will focus more on relationships, family, or personal growth and the remainder will be spread on the remaining life areas. What matters is not that all areas receive equal attention at all times, but that none of them are consistently abandoned or ignored over long periods of time.

This framework also helps explain why people often feel overwhelmed when they lack a clear vision of success across all five areas. When someone only develops a vision in one or a few life areas, responsibilities in the neglected areas tend to feel like unrelated chores instead of meaningful steps toward a larger purpose. One example would be the person who only has a vision in the social/hobbies life area. For them, professional discipline, relationship maintenance, parenting responsibilities, or spiritual growth can begin to feel intrusive and exhausting because they are experienced as interruptions to obtaining immediate social comfort. They are blinded to the fact that the other responsibilities are a necessary part of building a meaningful life.

By contrast, when a person has developed a clear vision across all 5 life areas, many of the non-social responsibilities feel more purposeful and coherent. The actions themselves may still be difficult, but they are no longer experienced as random extra demands. They are connected to something meaningful, which changes how they are interpreted and approached over time.

As you begin to apply the concepts from the Adversity Cycle and the confidence-building process, these five life areas give you a practical way to approach it. They allow you to identify meaningful goals, recognize where real adversity exists, and begin engaging with it in a way that produces measurable progress. You do not need to take on everything at once, but you do need to remain aware of all five areas and intentionally engage with them over time. As confidence begins to develop across these different parts of life, the overall direction of your life begins to shift in a way that is both more stable and more sustainable.

If you were to map this out visually, it would look something like Figure 2.

Applying the Five Life Areas

Understanding the five areas conceptually is important, but it becomes much more useful when you begin to see how it applies in real life. This is where Alex's situation becomes much clearer.

When we began looking at his life through this framework, it quickly became obvious that his struggles were not isolated to a single issue. They were spread across multiple life areas, and in some cases entire life areas had been left largely undeveloped. What initially appeared to be an isolated case of anxiety, depression and suicidal thoughts was actually connected to a much larger pattern of avoidance, underdevelopment, and imbalance across several life domains.

In his professional life, there was very little foundation to build on. Even basic expectations felt overwhelming because he had not yet developed the ability to consistently interact with others, tolerate discomfort, or follow through on responsibilities in a structured environment. Situations that most adults would consider manageable often felt paralyzing to him because he had spent so little time engaging with those kinds of demands. Instead of moving toward those limitations and developing the skills required to overcome them, he tended to avoid situations that exposed them.

In the area of romantic relationships, there was essentially no meaningful development at all. This was not because he lacked interest or desire, but because the foundational skills required for connection had not yet been established. Without the ability to consistently engage socially, tolerate discomfort, communicate effectively, and maintain healthy relationships in general, forming and sustaining a romantic relationship was not a realistic starting point. That area of his life remained largely undeveloped because the underlying foundations required for it had not yet been built elsewhere.

His social life was where the work initially needed to begin, but it was also where avoidance was strongest. Most of his interactions occurred in environments that allowed him to remain comfortable and avoid the kinds of real-world social challenges that require adaptation and growth. Online interactions, video games, and highly controlled environments allowed him to experience some level of connection without requiring the same degree of vulnerability, accountability, or social adjustment that face-to-face relationships require. Because he had not consistently engaged in situations where he needed to read other people, respond in real time, tolerate awkwardness, and adjust his behavior, the skills required for meaningful relationships had not developed.

At the same time, the social and hobbies life area had become disproportionately dominant in his life because it was one of the few places where he could still experience some level of feeling heard, seen, and appreciated without confronting the same level of adversity required in the other areas. He experienced moments of connection, excitement, novelty, and enjoyment, which created the illusion that things were functioning better than they actually were. In reality, he was trying to use those experiences as a substitute for growth in the other areas that were being consistently avoided.

Hobbies were one of the few places where he felt some level of competence and relief. He had activities that he enjoyed and could engage in without feeling constantly overwhelmed. While this provided temporary comfort, it also created a subtle trap. Because this area felt easier and safer, it became the default place he spent time and energy, which made it easier to continue avoiding the areas that required growth. Over time, this reinforced the imbalance rather than correcting it.

The spiritual and ethical area was one life area that had never been clearly defined. He had not spent much time thinking about what kind of person he wanted to become, what standards he wanted to live by, or what responsibilities came with becoming a capable adult. Decisions were often made based on what felt easiest, safest, or most immediately comforting rather than on a consistent set of values connected to the type of man he wanted to become. Without that framework, it became much more difficult for him to evaluate his own behavior honestly or consistently move toward the things that would let him feel like a person living in an ethical way.

When you look at these areas together, the pattern becomes much clearer. It was not that Alex was failing in one isolated way. It was that multiple areas of his life had been left underdeveloped, while the areas that provided immediate comfort and relief gradually became overemphasized. This imbalance allowed him to temporarily avoid discomfort, but also led to his struggles with anxiety, depression and suicidal thoughts. It also prevented him from developing the skills, confidence, discipline, and resilience needed to function in the real world.

This pattern is not unique to Alex. Many people will recognize parts of themselves in this framework. There are often areas of life where things feel manageable and others where engagement has been consistently avoided. The natural tendency is to spend more time in the areas that feel easiest while postponing the areas that feel uncomfortable, overwhelming, or emotionally exposing. Over time, however, that imbalance creates the same outcome: reduced confidence, increased anxiety, discouragement, instability, worsening depression, a growing sense of being stuck and in severe cases, suicidal thoughts.

This is also one of the reasons some people constantly feel overwhelmed by what appear to be normal adult responsibilities. When a clear vision of success has not been developed across all five life areas, responsibilities related to work, relationships, parenting, discipline, or personal growth begin to feel like endless extra chores rather than meaningful parts of building a fulfilling life. The imbalanced individual often remains heavily focused on immediate comfort, novelty, stimulation, or social validation while experiencing the responsibilities required for long-term growth as exhausting interruptions.

By contrast, people who have developed a meaningful vision across all five life areas tend to experience many of the same responsibilities very differently. The tasks themselves are not necessarily easier, but they are less overwhelming because they are connected to a larger purpose. Parenting, maintaining relationships, improving professionally, developing discipline, and growing ethically are not experienced as unrelated burdens. They are understood as part of becoming the kind of person capable of building the life they actually want.

The goal of understanding this pattern is not to criticize yourself or other people. It is to recognize what is happening clearly enough that you can make a plan to attack and overcome anxiety, depression or suicidal thoughts. Once you can identify where growth is occurring, where avoidance is occurring, and where imbalance exists, you can begin making more intentional decisions about where engagement is needed.

This is also where it becomes clear that meaningful change does not come from staying within the areas that already feel comfortable or familiar. It comes from gradually engaging with the areas that have been avoided, even when that engagement initially feels difficult or overwhelming. As that happens, the same process we discussed earlier begins to take place. Small actions lead to progress, progress builds confidence, and over time that confidence begins to expand into other areas of life.

The bottom line is this. When a person "down arrows" by avoiding multiple life areas at the same time, the impact compounds, and this is often when people begin to experience the level of anxiety, depression, hopelessness, and even suicidal thinking that feels overwhelming and impossible to escape. By contrast, a person "up arrows" by confronting challenges consistently across the 5 life areas, even in small ways, the overall direction of life begins to shift to more happiness and success. That shift does not happen all at once, and it does not require perfection in every area, but it does require a willingness to engage where growth is needed rather than continuing to avoid it.

Chapter 2 Summary

- Confidence is not something you are born with; it is built through repeated engagement with adversity over time.
- Real change begins when behavior changes in a measurable way, even if the first steps are small and uncomfortable.
- Healthy psychological functioning requires both meaningful accomplishment and healthy social connection, including feeling heard, seen, and appreciated.
- A clear vision of success across the major areas of life is necessary for creating meaningful goals that lead to growth rather than short-term comfort.
- Avoidance creates imbalance across life areas, reduces confidence and self-esteem, and contributes to increasing anxiety, depression, hopelessness, and suicidal thinking over time.
- Breaking life into five areas—professional, romantic, family, social/hobbies, and spiritual/ethical—provides a practical framework for identifying where growth is needed and where engagement has been avoided.

5 LIFE AREAS
PROFESSIONAL
ROMANTIC
FAMILY
SOCIAL & HOBBIES
SPRITUAL & ETHICS

Figure 2

CHAPTER 3

Living in the Up Arrow and Down Arrow

Up Arrow and Down Arrow

If you look closely at the moments we just described, a simple pattern starts to emerge. Every time you are faced with something uncomfortable or challenging, you move in one of two directions. You either move toward it, or you move away from it. These two directions are what determine whether you build capacity or continue reinforcing the patterns that keep you stuck.

When you move toward something that is uncomfortable, you are engaging with it. You stay present, you tolerate the discomfort, and you allow yourself to experience what is actually happening. That does not mean you handle it perfectly. It does not mean you say the right thing or make the best decision every time. It simply means that you do not avoid it. You remain in the situation long enough to learn from it, adjust, and begin building the ability to navigate similar situations in the future. This is what I refer to as an "up arrow."

When you move away from something that is uncomfortable, you are avoiding it. That avoidance can take many different forms. It can be obvious, such as leaving a situation, delaying a task, or refusing to engage. It can also be subtle, such as changing the subject, making a joke to deflect, rationalizing your behavior, or mentally checking out when things become difficult. In each case, the function is the same. You are creating distance between yourself and the discomfort. This is what I refer to as a down arrow.

At first, the difference between these two directions may not seem significant. In the moment, a down arrow often feels easier. It reduces discomfort quickly, and because of that, it can feel like the right choice. An up arrow, on the other hand, often feels harder. It requires effort, it may involve embarrassment or uncertainty, and it does not provide immediate relief. Because of that, it is easy to underestimate how important these decisions are.

What makes these choices powerful is not what happens in a single moment, but what happens when they are repeated. Each time you choose an up arrow, you are building the ability to handle similar situations in the future. Each time you choose a down arrow, you are reinforcing the belief that you cannot. Over time, those choices accumulate and begin to shape how you experience your life. As those patterns accumulate, they begin shaping not only behavior, but emotional experience as well. Repeated down arrows often contribute to increasing anxiety, discouragement, reduced self-esteem, and eventually the hopelessness many people experience as anxiety and depression.

This was something that became very clear with Alex as we started paying attention to these moments more closely. When he felt uncomfortable in therapy, his instinct was to move away from it by deflecting, explaining, or disengaging. Those responses made sense to him in the moment, but they also prevented him from learning anything new. When he began to recognize those patterns and, even occasionally, chose to stay in the conversation instead of escaping it, something started to shift. Those small moments of engagement did not immediately feel like major victories, but they were up arrows, and over time they began to change his ability to handle discomfort.

It is also important to understand that up arrows do not require perfection. You can struggle, say the wrong thing, or feel completely unsure of yourself and still be moving in the right direction. What matters is that you remain engaged and learn from the unsuccessful attempts to overcome the challenge. In many cases, the most important step is simply not leaving the situation when everything in you wants to escape it. That is often where the learning begins.

Down arrows are not always obvious, and they are not always intentional. Many people are not aware that they are avoiding something because the behavior feels justified. It can feel reasonable to explain why something is not your fault, to shift attention away from yourself, or to disengage from a situation that feels uncomfortable. The problem is not the justification. The problem is the direction it moves you. Even when it feels reasonable, avoidance still prevents growth and reinforces the same patterns over time.

As you begin to recognize these two directions, you will start to see them everywhere. They show up in conversations, in decisions, in habits, and in how you respond to stress. You will begin to notice moments where you instinctively move away from something and moments where you are uncomfortable but choose to stay engaged. That awareness is what allows you to begin responding differently, because you can only change a pattern you see.

This is not about labeling yourself as doing things right or wrong. It is about recognizing the direction of your responses and understanding what those responses are building over time. Every moment of discomfort presents an opportunity to move in one of these two directions, and over time, those decisions determine whether you develop the capacity to handle your life or continue reinforcing the patterns that creates anxiety, depression or suicidal thoughts.

You Are Already Doing This

Most people think of change as something that happens during major moments, when a big decision is made or when life forces them to confront something significant. While those moments do matter, they are not where most change actually happens. The direction of your life is shaped much more by the smaller decisions you make throughout the day, many of which are not noticed in the moment or considered insignificant.

From the time you wake up to the time you go to bed, you are constantly responding to what is in front of you and your responses make a big difference to your long-term growth and development. Some of those situations are obvious, but many are subtle. A conversation is safe but becomes uncomfortable, and you must decide whether to stay engaged or change the subject. A task feels overwhelming, and you choose whether to start it or delay it. Someone gives you feedback, and you decide whether to consider it or put up defenses. These moments may seem insignificant on their own, but they are not. They are the points where direction is determined.

What makes this difficult to recognize is that these decisions often happen quickly and feel automatic. Most people are not consciously thinking about whether they are engaging or avoiding. They are simply reacting in ways that have become familiar over time. Those reactions can feel justified in the moment, especially when they reduce discomfort, but they still move you in a specific direction. Over time, those small movements add up and begin to shape how people experience life.

This was happening with Alex long before he understood it. In therapy, there were many moments where a question or observation would make him uncomfortable, and his first instinct was to "down arrow" by shifting the focus away from himself. Sometimes that meant making a joke, sometimes it meant explaining why something was not his fault, other times it meant redirecting the conversation entirely, and at times dissociating into a dreamlike state. None of those responses felt like major decisions, and in the moment, they were easy to justify. But each of those moments still represented a choice in how he responded to what was in front of him.

As we began to slow those moments down and look at them more carefully, it became clear that what felt like a natural reaction was actually part of a "down arrow" pattern. When something felt uncomfortable, he moved away from it. That response made sense given his past, but it also meant he was repeatedly missing opportunities to learn, adjust, and grow. The same opportunities exist in our everyday life.

Most people are not making one large decision that determines their outcome. They are making many small decisions that, over time, create a consistent direction of either "up arrows" or "down arrows".

The important point here is not that you need to become aware of every single decision you make. That would be unrealistic and overwhelming. The point is that you are already engaged in this process, whether you recognize it or not. You are already responding to challenges, already choosing how to handle discomfort, and already moving in a direction based on those choices. The difference is that once you begin to see it, you have the ability to respond more intentionally instead of relying on patterns that may not be serving you.

This is where small "up arrow" moments begin to take on a different meaning. It is no longer something that only happens when you feel ready or when the situation is extreme. It becomes something that is available in the smaller moments that make up your daily life. Each of those moments gives you an opportunity to either continue reinforcing the patterns that have been keeping you stuck or begin moving in a different direction.

What It Feels Like in the Moment

Understanding the difference between moving toward something and moving away from it is one thing. Recognizing it in the moment is something entirely different. The challenge is that these decisions rarely present themselves clearly. They do not show up labeled as "up arrow" or "down arrow." Instead, they show up as feelings, thoughts, and impulses that seem reasonable at the time.

When you are in one of these moments, it usually does not feel like a decision about growth. It feels like discomfort. It might feel like embarrassment when someone points something out that you did not see. It might feel like frustration when something is harder than you expected. It might feel like anxiety when you are unsure how you are being perceived or how a situation is going to unfold. In those moments, your mind will often move quickly to reduce that discomfort, and the ways it does that can feel justified.

You may find yourself explaining why something is not your fault. You may focus on what the other person did wrong. You may tell yourself that the situation is not worth your time or that it does not matter. You may shift the conversation, change the subject, or mentally disengage. None of these responses feel like avoidance in the moment. They feel like protecting yourself, maintaining control, or responding appropriately to what is happening.

This is what makes these moments difficult to recognize. The behavior itself is not always obvious, and the reasoning behind it often feels valid. If someone reacts negatively, it can feel reasonable to conclude that they are the problem. If something is uncomfortable, it can feel logical to step away from it. Each of these responses reduces discomfort in the short term, which reinforces the pattern and makes it more likely to happen again.

This was happening repeatedly with Alex as he began to engage more in therapy. When something was pointed out that he had not seen before, his immediate reaction was often to explain why that was not what he intended or to redirect the focus to something else. In those moments, he did not experience himself as avoiding. He experienced himself as clarifying or defending his perspective. It felt justified, and because it felt justified, it was easy to continue doing it without recognizing the impact and he wasn't able to learn from that experience.

As we slowed those moments down, a different pattern began to emerge. He learned that the discomfort he was feeling was not coming from being attacked. It was coming from being exposed to something he had not yet learned how to handle. The instinct to explain, deflect, or disengage was not solving the problem. It was preventing him from understanding it. When he began to stay in those moments instead of escaping them, even when it felt uncomfortable, he started to see things he had not seen before.

This is where the experience of an up arrow begins to change. It does not suddenly feel easy or natural. In many cases, it still feels uncomfortable. The difference is that instead of reacting immediately to remove that discomfort, you begin to tolerate it long enough to understand what is happening. That shift may only last a few seconds at first, but those seconds matter because they create the space where learning can occur and where a different response becomes possible.

Down arrows, on the other hand, tend to feel immediate and relieving. The discomfort decreases quickly, and the situation feels resolved even though nothing has actually changed. That relief is what reinforces the pattern. Over time, the brain begins to associate avoidance with safety, even when that avoidance is creating larger problems in the background.

As you start to recognize these patterns more clearly, you will notice that the most important moments are not the ones that feel dramatic. They are the small points where you are about to react in a familiar and automatic way. The moment before you change the subject, the moment before you dismiss feedback, and the moment before you decide not to engage are the points where direction is determined and where your response begins to shape what happens next.

Learning to recognize those moments does not mean you will handle them perfectly. There will still be times where your emotions will get the best of you and you will quickly or move away from something before you fully realize what is happening. This is not the end of the world because the goal is not perfection. The goal is awareness, because as that awareness increases, you create more opportunities to respond differently, even if those changes are small at first.

Over time, those small changes begin to accumulate and your understanding will deepen. The moments where you stay engaged will become more frequent. The time you are able to tolerate discomfort will begin to increase. Situations that once triggered an immediate reaction begin to feel more manageable, not because the situations themselves have changed, but because your ability to remain present has improved and your responses propel you in a different direction.

Hurt Is Not Harm

One of the biggest obstacles to changing from an automatic down arrow to a conscious up arrow, is not a lack of understanding or even a lack of effort. It is a misunderstanding of what we are actually experiencing in those difficult moments. Many people have learned, often without realizing it, to interpret any form of emotional discomfort as something negative, something to be avoided, or a signal that something is wrong. This is not always accurate. In the way I teach this, I refer to that experience as hurt, because it is easier to recognize and remember. The problem is that hurt and harm are not the same thing, and when they are treated as if they are, people begin avoiding the very experiences that are necessary for growth.

Hurt is the temporary emotional pain that comes from facing something difficult. It is the feeling of being challenged, exposed, uncertain, or pushed beyond what is familiar. Harm, on the other hand, involves something that actually impairs your ability to grow, develop, or reach your true potential. The distinction between these two is critical, because if you interpret hurt as harm, you will consistently move away from uncomfortable situations that are necessary for growth, development and improvement.

This distinction is not always obvious in the moment. When something hurts emotionally, the body reacts quickly. You may feel tension, anxiety, embarrassment, or a strong urge to escape the situation. Those reactions can make it seem as if something damaging is happening, even when it is not. If you have learned to automatically trust that feeling as a signal that you are in danger and should leave, it becomes very difficult to stay engaged long enough to learn anything new. Many times, we hurt when there isn't an actual danger.

This was something Alex had to work through repeatedly in therapy. When feedback was given that challenged how he saw himself or how he had interacted with someone, the immediate reaction was hurt. Initially, that hurt was often perceived as rejection or attacking, even when the intention was to help him understand something he had missed. Because of that, his instinct was to defend himself, explain his intentions, or disengage from the conversation.

As we slowed those moments down and looked at them more carefully, it became clear that what he was experiencing was not harm. He was not being attacked, and he was not being rejected as a person. He was being exposed to information that was painful because it was unfamiliar and difficult to process. The hurt came from that exposure, not from actual damage. Instead of seeing hurt as a signal that something was wrong or that he had been attacked, he began to see it as a signal that he was in a place where learning could occur.

This distinction was important for Alex and remains important for all of us. Because many people incorrectly associate all hurt with being attacked, even when no actual harm has occurred, they will take inappropriate actions for their situation. When that inaccurate association is in place, the natural response is to move into a defensive position, to justify, explain, or push back against what is being said. In those moments, the focus shifts away from understanding and toward protecting oneself from a perceived threat. This generally damages social and romantic connections.

Over time, this pattern can make it difficult to engage in healthy confrontation or honest communication. Situations that are intended to provide feedback, resolve conflict, or improve understanding are instead incorrectly experienced as personal attacks. As a result, opportunities for growth are missed, not because the person is unwilling to improve, but because the experience itself is being misinterpreted. In healthy relationships, growth often requires moments of discomfort, disagreement, criticism, correction, or confrontation. These experiences may hurt emotionally, but that does not mean they are harmful. In many cases, they are necessary for deeper understanding, stronger relationships, and long-term growth.

Learning to recognize that hurt does not automatically mean harm, and does not automatically mean that you are being attacked, is what allows you to stay engaged in those moments long enough to learn from them. That shift does not eliminate the hurt. In many cases, it still feels just as strong. What changes is how you interpret it, how you respond to it and the learning you gain from staying engaged.

Instead of reacting immediately to eliminate the discomfort, you begin to tolerate it long enough to understand what is happening and decide how to respond. That pause, even if it is brief, creates the opportunity to choose a more productive response that is more likely to reduce the risk of anxiety, depression and suicidal thoughts. This is where the process described in the previous sections begins to come together. The moment of hurt becomes the moment where a decision is made. Moving away from it reinforces the patterns that have been keeping you stuck. Moving toward it, even in a small way, creates the conditions for learning, growth, and increased confidence over time.

Accumulation in Real Time

At this point, the distinction between moving toward something and moving away from it, and the difference between hurt and harm, begin to connect in a way that should be more practical. What makes these ideas powerful is not what happens in any single moment, but what happens when those moments begin to accumulate over time. Each individual decision may feel small, but together they create a pattern that becomes increasingly difficult to ignore.

Most people are not making one decision that determines if they constantly struggle with anxiety and depression. They are making many small decisions, often throughout the same day, that make that determination. When those decisions consistently move away from what is difficult, the pattern becomes one of avoidance, and over time that avoidance leads to problems building up. When those decisions consistently move toward what is difficult, the pattern becomes one of engagement, and over time that engagement builds capacity, confidence, and self-esteem.

This accumulation is what explains why change can feel slow at first and then begin to accelerate. Early in the process, the differences between moving toward something and moving away from it may not be obvious. A single conversation, a single decision, or a single attempt may not seem to change much. However, those moments are not isolated. They are adding to a larger pattern, and as that pattern develops, the impact becomes more noticeable.

This was evident in the way things unfolded for Alex. At the beginning, his efforts did not look dramatic. Showing up to therapy, staying in uncomfortable conversations, and beginning to reflect on his own behavior did not immediately change his circumstances. From the outside, it might have appeared that very little was happening. What was not obvious at the time was that those small moments were beginning to accumulate.

As that accumulation continued, the effects became clearer. He started to recognize patterns in his behavior that he had not seen before. He became more aware of how he was communicating with others and how those interactions were being perceived. That awareness created opportunities to adjust, and each adjustment added to his ability to handle similar situations in the future. When he applied those changes outside of therapy, the results were not perfect, but they were different. He was able to stay engaged in situations that he would have previously avoided, and that engagement began to produce real-world consequences.

His early experiences in a work environment reflected this process. The first time he attempted to function in that setting, the same patterns that had caused difficulty in therapy showed up again. Social interactions felt awkward, communication was inconsistent, and the environment became uncomfortable for both him and the people around him. Eventually, that situation did not work out, and he lost that opportunity. In the past, that experience would have likely reinforced his tendency to seek future employment. Instead, the process continued.

He quickly sought out and found another job but this time he was not starting from the same place. The work he had done in therapy had already begun to change how he responded to coworker and professional requirements. While there were still challenges, he was able to stay engaged longer, adjust more effectively, and handle situations that would have previously caused him to withdraw. That led to a different outcome, not because the situation itself was easier, but because his ability to navigate it had improved.

Over time, this pattern continued to build. Each experience added to his ability to handle what was in front of him, and each adjustment made future situations more manageable. What started as small, often uncomfortable moments in therapy eventually translated into greater stability in his daily life. The changes were not immediate, and they were not perfect, but they were consistent, and that consistency is what allowed the pattern to shift.

This is how the direction of your life changes in real time. It does not happen all at once, and it does not require a single defining moment. It happens through repeated engagement with the situations that are already present in your life. Each time you move toward what is difficult, you are adding to a pattern that builds your ability to handle more. Each time you move away, you are reinforcing a pattern that limits that ability. Over time, those patterns become increasingly clear in the way you experience your life.

What makes this both challenging and encouraging is that the process is always active. You are always adding to one pattern or the other. That means that change is not something that is only available in rare or extreme circumstances. It is available in the smaller moments that occur throughout your day. Recognizing those moments and responding to them differently is what allows the accumulation to begin working in your favor instead of against you.

As this accumulation continues, something important begins to happen. The effort required to stay engaged starts to feel more manageable. Situations that once triggered an immediate desire to avoid begin to feel like something you can handle, even if they are still uncomfortable. That shift is not the result of the situation becoming easier. It is the result of you becoming more capable through repeated engagement.

As this process continues, confidence and self-esteem begin to grow as more evidence accumulates that you are capable of handling what life requires. Over time, situations that once felt overwhelming begin to feel more manageable, not because life has stopped being difficult, but because your ability to engage with it has changed.

This is the point where the pattern begins to sustain itself. What initially required a great deal of effort begins to feel more natural, and the direction you are moving becomes more consistent. While there will still be moments where you choose to avoid or where things do not go as planned, the overall pattern begins to favor growth rather than stagnation. That shift, built over time through many small decisions, is what ultimately changes the trajectory of your life.

Chapter 3 Summary

- Consciously or not, you are constantly making small decisions to either move toward (up arrow) or away from (down arrow) what is difficult, often without realizing it.
- Up arrows require you to stay engaged in discomfort long enough to learn and build capacity, while down arrows reduce discomfort in the moment but prevent growth.
- What feels like protection in the moment is often avoidance, and repeated avoidance reinforces the patterns that keep you stuck.
- Hurt is not the same as harm; discomfort is often a necessary part of learning and does not mean you are being attacked.
- Change happens through the accumulation of small decisions over time, not through a single defining moment.
- As you consistently engage rather than avoid, your ability to handle life improves, and the direction of your life begins to shift.

CHAPTER 4

What Avoidance Actually Looks Like

As we briefly mentioned earlier, most people think about avoidance as something obvious but this isn't always the case. People picture avoidance as always being someone refusing to show up, walking away from a responsibility, or clearly disengaging from something that needs to be addressed. While those forms of avoidance do exist, they are not the most common ways it shows up in everyday life. Most avoidance is much more subtle, and because of that, it is much harder to recognize. Because it is so important to understand deeply, we will briefly repeat some very important principles and expound on others.

Avoidance often feels reasonable in the moment. It does not usually present itself as a clear decision to move away from something important. Instead, it shows up as a reaction that seems justified based on what you are experiencing. If something feels uncomfortable, it can seem logical to step back. If a situation feels frustrating, it can feel appropriate to focus on what the other person is doing wrong. If you feel uncertain, it can feel safer to delay action until you feel more prepared. In each case, the response makes sense on the surface, which is why it is so easy to continue without questioning it.

This is what makes avoidance difficult to identify. It rarely feels like avoidance when it is happening. It feels like protecting yourself, maintaining control, or responding appropriately to the situation in front of you. Because of that, people can spend long periods of time reinforcing avoidance patterns without ever recognizing that they are doing it. The behavior blends into normal decision-making, and the long-term impact remains largely invisible until the consequences begin to accumulate. This is called Habituation.

In some cases, avoidance is even interpreted as a positive trait. People who consistently move away from discomfort are often described as "easygoing" or as someone who "goes with the flow." While this may appear to reflect flexibility or calmness, it can also frequently signal a pattern of disengaging from situations that require effort, confrontation, or intentional growth. Over time, this can quietly limit development across multiple areas of life while still appearing reasonable on the surface. These individuals will often struggle with levels of anxiety and depression.

This pattern was present in many of Alex's interactions, both inside and outside of therapy. When something felt uncomfortable, his instinct was not to disengage in an obvious way, but to respond in ways that allowed him to avoid the discomfort while still appearing engaged. He might shift the conversation, explain his intentions, or focus on something external that seemed more relevant in the moment. From his perspective, he was participating in the conversation. In reality, he was moving away from the difficult parts of the interaction that would have allowed him to learn and improve.

One of the reasons this type of avoidance is so effective is that it often preserves a sense of consistency in how someone sees themselves. If a situation is reframed in a way that removes personal responsibility, there is no need to confront the possibility that they need to change in order to heal from anxiety, depression or overcome suicidal thoughts. If someone else can be identified as the source of the problem, the discomfort can be resolved without requiring any adjustment in their own behavior. This allows the individual to maintain their current perspective while avoiding the effort and uncertainty that comes with growth.

This pattern was not limited to Alex's own behavior. There were also situations where the discomfort he experienced was quickly reduced by others around him stepping in to make things easier. While those responses were well-intentioned, they often reduced opportunities for him to engage directly with the situations that would have required growth.

Understanding this broader pattern is important because it highlights how avoidance can become embedded in multiple layers of a person's life. It is not always a single decision or a single behavior. It is often a system of responses that all serve the same function, which is to reduce discomfort in the short term. Over time, those responses create a pattern that moves someone further away from the situations that would allow them to grow.

The challenge is that as long as avoidance feels justified, it remains invisible. It is only when you begin to look more closely at the function of your behavior, rather than the reasoning behind it, that the pattern becomes clear. When you shift your focus from "Does this make sense?" to "What direction is this moving me in?" you begin to see avoidance for what it is, even when it appears reasonable on the surface, and that shift in perspective is what allows you to begin recognizing and addressing these patterns more directly.

Why Avoidance Happens

To understand why avoidance is so persistent, it helps to look at what it actually does in the moment. Avoidance is not random, and it is not a sign that someone lacks intelligence or insight. It is a response that serves a very specific function. As I explain in my previous work "Conquering PTSD," avoidance in the short term reduces hurt. When something feels uncomfortable, uncertain, or exposing, moving away from it creates immediate temporary relief but with long term consequences. That relief may be brief, but it is real, and because it is real, it reinforces the behavior that produced it.

This is what makes avoidance so difficult to change. The brain learns quickly that certain responses lead to a temporary reduction in emotional discomfort. If explaining, deflecting, disengaging, or delaying produces even a small decrease in that feeling, the brain begins to incorrectly associate those behaviors with long term safety. Over time, those responses become more automatic, and the individual is less likely to question them because they have been reinforced repeatedly.

The problem is that while avoidance reduces hurt in the moment, that part of the brain does not realize that avoidance does not resolve what created that hurt in the first place or understand the long-term consequences that avoidance created. Additionally, the skill needed to avoid repeating this situation has not been developed, and the underlying issue is still present. In many cases, the situation that created the initial discomfort becomes more likely because the initial cause has not been addressed. This creates a pattern where short-term relief leads to long-term limitation, and that limitation then creates more situations that feel uncomfortable, which increases the likelihood of further avoidance. Over time, this pattern often contributes to increasing anxiety, reduced confidence, discouragement, and the hopelessness many people experience as depression or suicidal thoughts.

This pattern was very clear in Alex's experience. When something in therapy felt uncomfortable, his instinct was to explain why it was not his fault or to shift the focus away from himself. In those moments, that response reduced the immediate discomfort. It allowed him to maintain his perspective without having to consider any other perspectives, and for a brief period, the situation felt resolved. However, nothing had actually changed. The same patterns would show up again, and the same discomfort would return, often with greater intensity because it had not been addressed the first time.

As he began to recognize this, it became easier to see that the relief he was experiencing was temporary and that it came at a cost. Each time he avoided the situation, he was reinforcing the belief that he could not handle it. That belief made future situations feel more overwhelming, which increased the urge to avoid them. Over time, the pattern became self-reinforcing. Avoidance led to increased difficulty, and increased difficulty led to more avoidance.

This same process can occur in relationships as well. When someone steps in and removes discomfort for another person, both individuals often experience relief in the moment. The person struggling no longer has to confront the difficulty, and the person helping no longer has to watch them struggle. While this response is understandable and often comes from a place of care, it can reinforce the same avoidance pattern by removing opportunities for engagement and growth.

Understanding this helps explain why avoidance is not simply a personal weakness or a lack of effort. It is a learned response that has been reinforced over time, often in ways that made sense in the moment. The goal is not to eliminate that response entirely, but to recognize when it is happening and understand what it is doing. When you can see that avoidance is providing short-term relief while creating long-term difficulty, it becomes easier to question whether that trade-off is worth it. Conversely, when you can see the discomfort will stop growth, you can step in to help carry some of the load.

This is where the distinction between hurt and harm becomes especially important. If hurt is interpreted as harm, then avoidance will always feel justified. If hurt is recognized as a temporary and necessary part of growth, then staying engaged becomes a more viable option. The situation itself may not change, but your ability to remain in it long enough to learn and adjust begins to improve.

As this understanding develops, avoidance starts to become more visible. The behaviors themselves may not change immediately, but your awareness of them increases. You begin to notice when you are explaining instead of reflecting, when you are disengaging instead of staying present, and when you are delaying instead of taking action. That awareness creates the opportunity to respond differently, even if those changes are small at first.

Over time, this shift in awareness begins to interrupt the automatic nature of avoidance. What once felt like the only option begins to feel like a choice, and that choice becomes the point where change can occur.

Avoidance in Relationships

As we alluded to above, avoidance does not only occur within an individual. It often becomes embedded in relationships, especially in situations where one person cares deeply about the well-being of another. In those moments, the instinct to protect can become just as powerful as the instinct to avoid, and while that instinct often comes from a good place, it can unintentionally create the same outcome.

When someone you care about is struggling, it is difficult to watch. Seeing another person experience hurt, frustration, failure, or uncertainty can create a strong emotional response, and the natural emotional impulse is often to step in and make things easier. Removing the source of discomfort can feel loving and supportive because it provides immediate relief not only for the person who is struggling, but also for the person witnessing the struggle.

The difficulty is that consistently removing discomfort can also remove the opportunity for growth. When someone is repeatedly protected from situations that require engagement, they lose opportunities to develop the skills, confidence, and resilience needed to handle similar situations in the future. Over time, this can create increasing dependence on others to manage what feels difficult or overwhelming.

This was part of what occurred in Alex's life. There were situations where others stepped in quickly to reduce his discomfort rather than allowing him to work through it himself. In the short term, those situations felt resolved. However, because the underlying challenges were never fully engaged, the same difficulties continued appearing later with similar or even greater intensity.

At the same time, it is important to recognize that these patterns rarely develop because people do not care. In many cases, they develop because people care deeply. Parents, partners, friends, and family members often step in because they genuinely want to help. The issue is not the intention behind the behavior. The issue is whether the savior understands the difference between hurt and harm and whether their rescue attempts support engagement or replaces it.

Over time, these dynamics can shape expectations within relationships in ways that are not always immediately obvious. When someone repeatedly experiences others stepping in to remove discomfort, they may begin to associate love as being shielded from difficulty. As a result, being allowed to experience normal stress, disagreement, confrontation, or emotional discomfort can incorrectly feel like evidence that they are not being supported or loved properly.

This leads to situations where one person increasingly expects inappropriate emotional protection while the other incorrectly feels responsible for managing or eliminating discomfort within the relationship. When that expectation is not met, conflict often increases because the situation is interpreted as a lack of care rather than as a normal part of growth, communication, or adult responsibility.

In this way, avoidance can become embedded within the relationship itself. The pattern no longer exists only inside the individual. It becomes part of the interaction between people, where both individuals unintentionally reinforce the same cycle even while trying to help each other.

This is why the distinction between support and avoidance becomes so important. Support provides encouragement, guidance, stability, and accountability while still allowing the individual to engage with what is difficult. Avoidance removes the engagement altogether. **When support replaces engagement, avoidance is reinforced. When support is combined with engagement, growth becomes possible.**

This difference may appear subtle in the moment, but over time it creates very different outcomes. Walking alongside someone as they struggle is very different from removing the struggle itself. In one situation, the individual is still required to adapt, learn, and grow. In the other, the opportunity for that growth is taken away.

Understanding this dynamic helps explain why avoidance can persist even in environments where people are genuinely trying to help. It is not simply a matter of individual choice. It is often a relational pattern reinforced through interactions, expectations, and responses that reduce discomfort in the short term while limiting growth in the long term.

Wild Cards

As avoidance becomes more ingrained, it does not always remain obvious. In many cases, it becomes more sophisticated. Instead of simply stepping away from discomfort, the individual begins using an identity to reinterpret situations in a way that removes the need to engage with them at all. This is what I refer to as a "wild card."

A wild card is a way of creating or attaching to an identity that changes the rules for a particular individual or group. Once those rules are changed, the identity is then used to demand the validation, understanding, or status associated with living up to certain expectations without actually having to consistently live by those same expectations.

Wild cards allow people to avoid confronting what is difficult by creating a façade of justification that permits them to step outside of normal accountability. In the moment, this does not feel like avoidance. It feels like standing up for oneself, protecting one's identity, or responding appropriately to what is happening. In reality, however, it often creates a double standard where the rules they expect others to follow no longer apply equally to themselves.

The deep emotional attachment people develop toward these identities is part of what makes wild cards so difficult to recognize. They are often built on reasoning that feels valid. A person may believe they are being treated unfairly, misunderstood, or disrespected, and those perceptions may contain elements of truth. However, the function of the response is what determines whether it is helpful. If the response removes the need to engage with what is actually happening, then it is still functioning as avoidance, even if the reasoning behind it feels justified.

One way this shows up is through the creation of exceptions. The individual begins operating under a different set of rules for themselves than they would apply to others. Behavior that would be considered unacceptable if done by someone else becomes acceptable when applied to themselves because it is supported by a justification that removes the need for accountability. This creates a situation where growth becomes limited, not because the individual is incapable of change, but because they have found a way to avoid the conditions that would require it.

In some cases, these justifications are tied to aspects of identity, life experience, or personal history. A person may rely on their background, role, past experiences, or characteristics such as gender, race, or personal circumstances as a way of explaining why certain expectations should not apply to them. In other situations, it may be connected to experiences of hardship, trauma, or roles they have held, such as being a veteran, a parent, or someone who has faced significant adversity in life.

It is important to be clear about what is happening in these moments. These factors may be real, and they may matter in meaningful ways, but they do not change the function of the down arrow response. If they are being used in a way that removes the need to engage with what is difficult, then they are still operating as a form of avoidance. The question is not whether the explanation contains elements of truth. The question is whether it is being used to move toward growth or to step away from it.

When this pattern combines with a wild card, avoidance is often reinforced by the belief that emotional discomfort itself is evidence that something unjust, unfair, or personally threatening is occurring. If feeling hurt is automatically interpreted as proof of being attacked, mistreated, or discriminated against, then situations that require growth can be dismissed without further examination. In those moments, the focus shifts away from understanding and toward defending against a perceived threat. The result is that the individual avoids engaging with the situation, even when that engagement is necessary for growth.

It is important to recognize that this does not mean the individual is intentionally trying to avoid growth. In most cases, the response feels automatic and justified. The goal is not to eliminate the reasoning, but to look more closely at what the response is doing. If the outcome of the response is that you are no longer required to engage with what is difficult, then it is functioning as a down arrow, regardless of how reasonable it may feel.

As you begin to recognize wild cards in your own thinking, it becomes easier to see how they magnify the same patterns we have been describing. They reduce discomfort in the moment, but they prevent the development of the skills needed to handle similar situations in the future. Over time, the wild card perpetuates the same outcome as the more obvious forms of avoidance but often to a much larger degree. Even though it may look very different on the surface, avoidance combined with a wild card often intensifies the same long-term patterns we have already discussed. Over time, this combination can significantly increase hopelessness, emotional instability, anxiety, depression, and even suicidal thinking because it removes many of the normal pressures that would otherwise push a person toward growth and accountability.

Understanding this allows you to ask a different question in those moments. Instead of asking whether your reaction feels justified because of a certain identity, you begin to ask whether your response is helping you move toward or away from what needs to be addressed. That shift in focus brings the decision back into the framework we have been building and makes it possible to choose a different direction.

Bringing It Together

What is important to recognize is that everything described in this chapter represents different forms of the same process within the Adversity Cycle. These are all examples of what it looks like to move away from discomfort rather than toward it. The specific behavior may vary from person to person, but the direction remains the same. Whether avoidance appears as disengagement, justification, emotional protection, reliance on others to remove discomfort, or more sophisticated forms like wild cards, each of these responses functions as a down arrow within the larger pattern we have been discussing.

The thing you need to take away from this chapter is that avoidance is not always obvious, and it is not always intentional, but it is consistent in what it does. Over time, these patterns create increasing distance between you and the very experiences that are necessary for growth. What reduces hurt in the short term often reinforces anxiety, worsens depression, reduced confidence, discouragement, and increases the risk of suicidal thoughts over time because it prevents engagement with the situations that would have allowed new skills, confidence, and resilience to develop.

What makes this challenging is that many of these responses feel reasonable in the moment. They reduce hurt, maintain a sense of control, and allow you to move past discomfort without having to fully engage with it. Because of that, it is easy to continue reinforcing these patterns without recognizing the long-term impact they are having. The short-term relief becomes the focus, while the long-term consequences remain out of view until they begin to accumulate.

This is why the distinction between moving toward something and moving away from it remains so important. Every form of avoidance, no matter how it presents itself, is a down arrow. It may look different on the surface, and it may feel justified based on the situation, but if it removes the need to engage with what is difficult, it is still moving you in the same direction. Over time, those repeated decisions shape your ability to handle your life in a very real way.

The same is true in the opposite direction. Each time you remain engaged, even when it is uncomfortable, clumsy or barely effective, you are building something that did not exist before. You are increasing your capacity to handle similar situations in the future, and that increase in capacity is what leads to confidence. The process is not always visible in the moment, but it becomes clear over time as your ability to navigate challenges begins to change and your mental health can improve.

This was evident in the shift that occurred for Alex. Early on, avoidance showed up in ways that felt natural and justified, and because of that, it continued without much awareness. As he began to recognize those patterns and respond differently, even in small ways, the direction of his behavior began to change. The situations themselves did not become easier, but his ability to stay engaged within them improved. That improvement created opportunities for growth that had not been present before, and over time, those opportunities began to change his experience in meaningful ways.

It is also important to recognize that this process does not happen in isolation. The way you respond to your own discomfort influences how others respond to you, and the way others respond to you can either reinforce avoidance or support engagement. When support replaces engagement, avoidance is reinforced. When support is combined with engagement, growth becomes possible. Understanding this dynamic allows you to recognize not only your own patterns, but also how those patterns are being supported or challenged within your environment.

As you begin to apply what you have learned in this chapter, the goal is not to handle every situation perfectly. The goal is to begin recognizing when avoidance is happening and to understand what it is doing. Once you can see that clearly, you can begin making different choices, even if those choices are small at first. Over time, those small changes accumulate and begin to shift the overall direction of your life.

The patterns described in this chapter are already active in your life. The difference moving forward is that you now have a way to recognize them. That awareness is what allows you to begin moving toward what is difficult instead of away from it, and that shift is what creates the foundation for everything that follows.

Chapter 4 Summary

- Avoidance is often subtle and feels justified, which makes it difficult to recognize in real time.
- Avoidance reduces hurt in the moment but reinforces anxiety, reduced confidence, and patterns that increase difficulty over time.
- Avoidance can occur within the individual and within relationships, especially when discomfort is consistently removed instead of worked through.
- More sophisticated forms of avoidance, such as creating exceptions or justifications for yourself, still function as down arrows even when they feel reasonable.
- When support replaces engagement, avoidance is reinforced, but when support is combined with engagement, growth becomes possible.

CHAPTER 5

Not All Stepping Away Is Avoidance

As Alex began to engage more consistently, a new pattern started to emerge that was not immediately obvious to him. When he experienced stress or discomfort between sessions, his instinct was to address it as quickly as possible. If something felt overwhelming, he would often want to reach out right away, sometimes multiple times in a short period, with the goal of resolving what he was feeling in that moment.

From his perspective, this made sense. He was no longer avoiding the problem. He was trying to deal with it. After spending so much time moving away from discomfort, it felt like progress to move toward it immediately. However, what he was actually doing was a different form of avoidance. He was still reacting to the discomfort itself and trying to remove it as quickly as possible rather than tolerating it long enough to clearly identify the problem, think through the best way to confront it, and determine whether the environment was appropriate to address it effectively.

Part of the work at that stage was helping him understand that not every experience of discomfort required an immediate response. In some situations, the more effective response was to slow down and give himself time to think clearly before acting. There were times where the most effective thing he could do was to wait, sit with what he was feeling, and bring it into the next session where it could be addressed more clearly and productively.

That shift was not easy. Waiting did not reduce the discomfort right away, and it often felt like he was doing less instead of more. In reality, however, he was beginning to build the ability to tolerate discomfort long enough to analyze the situation more accurately and choose a response that was better than the emotional reaction he initially wanted to have.

As that ability developed, something important began to change. Instead of needing to resolve every situation in the moment, he became able to hold onto discomfort long enough to think more clearly about what had happened and how he wanted to respond. That shift created space between the feeling and the reaction, and that space made it possible for him to engage more effectively when the time was right.

This is where people often become confused. As they begin to understand the importance of engaging with what is difficult, it can feel like the correct response is to confront everything immediately. If avoiding something keeps you stuck, then it seems logical that the solution would be to address every situation as soon as it appears. In practice, however, that approach can create its own problems.

Not every situation requires an immediate response, and not every moment is the right time to address what is happening. Moving away from something can look the same on the surface, but it does not always function in the same way. In some cases, stepping away is a form of avoidance, where the goal is to escape discomfort and avoid engagement altogether. In other cases, stepping away is intentional. It is a decision to pause, wait for a more appropriate time, or prepare for a more effective response.

While these two actions may appear similar, they lead to very different outcomes. Avoidance moves you away from what needs to be addressed. Delay, when used correctly, prepares you to move toward it in a more effective way. Understanding the difference between the two is what allows you to respond with greater intention instead of reacting automatically to what you are experiencing.

What Avoidance Is (and What It Isn't)

Before we can clearly understand what it means to delay effectively, we need to be precise about what avoidance actually is. Without that clarity, it becomes easy to mislabel behavior in a way that allows the same patterns to continue under a different name.

Avoidance is not defined by stepping away from something. It is defined by what happens after you step away. If the result of your response is that you do not return to engaging with what needs to be addressed, then it is avoidance, regardless of how reasonable the decision may have felt in the moment. Avoidance removes the need to deal with the situation altogether, and because of that, it prevents growth.

This is why avoidance can be difficult to recognize. It often feels justified. You may tell yourself that you need more time, that the situation is not important, or that it will resolve on its own. You may believe that you are choosing to "let it go" or that you are "avoiding unnecessary conflict." In some cases, those explanations may contain elements of truth, but the key issue is not whether the reasoning sounds reasonable. The key issue is whether the situation is actually being addressed.

When avoidance is present, the pattern is consistent. The situation remains unresolved, the underlying issue continues to exist, and the same challenges reappear over time. Each time this happens, it reinforces the belief that the situation is too difficult to handle, which increases the likelihood of avoiding it again in the future. Over time, this creates a cycle where avoidance leads to more difficulty, and more difficulty leads to more avoidance. Over time, this cycle often contributes to increasing anxiety, reduced confidence, discouragement, and the sense of being emotionally trapped that many people experience as depression.

This is something Alex had to confront as he began to change his behavior. Early in the process, there were many situations that he simply did not return to. Whether it was a social interaction that felt uncomfortable or a responsibility that felt overwhelming, his instinct was to move away and not come back to it. From his perspective, those decisions often felt reasonable. The discomfort was real, and stepping away provided relief. However, the situations themselves did not improve. They remained unresolved, and when they appeared again, they felt just as difficult, if not more so.

As he began to look at these patterns more closely, it became clear that the issue was not whether the situation was uncomfortable. The issue was whether he was actually engaging with it. When he avoided it, nothing changed. When he returned to it, even if it was difficult, there was at least an opportunity for something different to happen. That distinction became one of the clearest indicators of whether he was moving in a direction that would lead to growth.

Avoidance is not always immediate or obvious. It can take the form of delay without intention, where something is pushed off repeatedly without a clear plan to return to it. It can show up as distraction, where attention is redirected to something else that feels more manageable. It can appear as rationalization, where a convincing explanation is used to justify why engagement is not necessary. In each case, the outward behavior may look different, but the function is the same. The individual is moving away from what needs to be addressed.

Understanding avoidance in this way removes much of the confusion around it. It is not about whether you step away in a given moment. It is about whether you come back. If you do not return to engage with the situation, then the behavior is functioning as avoidance, regardless of how it is labeled. This clarity is what allows you to recognize the pattern more consistently and begin to respond differently.

What Delay Actually Is

Once you understand what avoidance is and how it functions, the next step is to clarify what it means to delay effectively. This is where many people become confused, because on the surface, avoidance and delay can look very similar. In both cases, you are stepping away from something in the moment. The difference is not what you do initially. The difference is what you intend to do next.

Avoidance is designed to remove the need to deal with the situation altogether. It creates distance without a plan to return, and because of that, the issue remains unresolved. Delay, when used correctly, serves a different purpose. It creates space so that you can engage more effectively at a later time. It is not a way of escaping the situation. It is a way of preparing to face it.

This distinction is what Alex had to learn as he continued to make progress. When discomfort arose, his instinct was often to resolve it immediately because he believed that immediate action meant effective action. What he was actually doing was reacting to the discomfort itself rather than engaging with the situation in a way that would lead to growth.

Part of the work at that stage was helping him understand that not every situation required an immediate response. There were times where the more effective action was to wait and bring the issue into the next session, where it could be addressed more clearly and productively. That shift was difficult because waiting did not reduce the discomfort right away. It required him to tolerate what he was feeling without immediately resolving it, which initially felt like doing less instead of doing more.

As he developed that ability, he began to create space between what he was experiencing and how he responded to it. That space allowed him to think more clearly about what had happened and engage with it more intentionally, which led to more effective interactions both in therapy and in his everyday life.

The key to this process is understanding that delay is not passive. It is an intentional decision that includes a plan to return. Without that plan, what appears to be delay quickly becomes avoidance. The question is not whether you step away from something in the moment. The question is whether you are preparing to engage with it or whether you are removing the need to do so.

There are three factors that determine whether a delay is effective or whether it is simply avoidance in a different form. When one or more of these factors are not aligned, stepping away can be the correct and more developed response. What matters is that the delay includes a clear intention to reengage under the right conditions.

• The appropriate time — Are you in a position to think clearly and respond intentionally, or are you reacting in the moment?
• The appropriate place — Is this an environment where the situation can be addressed productively, or are there distractions, pressures, or constraints that would interfere?
• The appropriate audience — Are you engaging with the right person, or are you bringing the issue to someone who cannot resolve it?

If any one of these factors is not aligned, delaying the response can be the more effective choice. Waiting for a more appropriate time, place, or audience is not avoidance when it is done with intention. It is a sign that you are taking the situation seriously enough to engage with it in a way that is more likely to lead to a productive outcome.

At the same time, delay only functions as growth when it includes a commitment to return. If there is no clear plan to reengage, then the delay becomes avoidance, even if it is described differently. The distinction is not whether you step away. It is whether you come back.

This is where a more developed response begins to emerge. An immediate reaction can feel productive because it creates a sense of action, but it is not always effective. A more intentional response considers whether the conditions are right for engagement and is willing to wait when they are not, while still maintaining responsibility for addressing the situation. That willingness to pause, without abandoning the issue, is what allows you to engage more effectively over time.

When Delay Becomes Avoidance

Once people begin to understand the idea of delay, a new challenge often appears. The same concept that allows for more effective engagement can also be used to justify continued avoidance. Without careful attention, it becomes easy to label something as delay when it is actually serving the same function as avoidance.

The difference between the two is not based on how the decision sounds, but on what follows. Delay includes a clear intention to return and engage with the situation under better conditions. Avoidance removes that intention and allows the situation to remain unresolved. When there is no plan to reengage, the behavior is not delay, regardless of how it is described.

This is where the pattern becomes subtle. A person may say they are waiting for the right time, but no specific time is ever identified. They may believe they are choosing a better place to address the issue, but they never create that opportunity. They may tell themselves that they will speak to the right person later, but the conversation never takes place. In each case, the language suggests intention, but the behavior reflects avoidance.

For delay to function as growth, it must include a clear plan for reengagement. That plan requires three elements: a specific time, a specific place, and a specific audience. If any of these are missing and there is no intention to define them, then what appears to be delay is functioning as avoidance.

- The appropriate time — When will you return to address this?

- The appropriate place — Where will this be handled in a way that allows for a productive outcome?
- The appropriate audience — Who is the correct person to engage with to resolve this?

If you are not identifying these three elements and committing to return, then you are not delaying. You are avoiding. The distinction is not based on how the decision feels in the moment. It is based on whether you take responsibility for reengaging with the situation under the right conditions.

This is something Alex had to learn as he began to improve. There were moments where stepping away was appropriate, but only when it was paired with a clear plan to return. Without that structure, it would have been easy to continue postponing situations that felt uncomfortable while believing that he was handling them effectively. What allowed him to continue progressing was not simply stepping away, but consistently returning and engaging in a way that created movement.

Another way that avoidance pretends to be delay is in the belief that more preparation is always needed before action. A person may feel that they need to think it through more, gather more information, or wait until they feel more confident before engaging. While preparation can be useful, it becomes avoidance when it delays action without leading to engagement. At some point, preparation must transition into action, or it serves the same function as avoidance.

This is why it is not enough to ask whether stepping away feels reasonable. The more important question is whether it leads back to appropriate engagement. If it does, then it is a sign of maturing into someone who knows when to delay. If it does not, then it is functioning as avoidance, even if it feels intentional in the moment. Learning to recognize this difference requires honesty and consistency, because the pattern will often present itself in ways that feel justified but ultimately prevent growth.

Applying the Distinction

At this point, the distinction between avoidance and delay should be clearer. The challenge moving forward is not simply understanding the difference, but applying it consistently in real situations. This is where the concepts in this chapter begin to take on practical value, because the decisions you make in these moments determine whether you continue reinforcing old patterns or begin moving in a different direction.

In everyday life, situations rarely present themselves in a controlled or ideal way. Conversations happen unexpectedly, stress builds at inconvenient times, and challenges often appear when you are not fully prepared to deal with them. In those moments, the goal is not to respond perfectly. The goal is to recognize what is happening and make a decision that moves you toward engagement rather than away from it.

This is where the distinction between avoidance and delay becomes a tool rather than just an idea. When something difficult comes up, you are no longer limited to reacting automatically. You can ask yourself whether the situation is being avoided or whether it is being postponed with the intention to address it more effectively. That question alone creates a pause, and that pause is where more intentional decisions begin to take shape.

There will be times where engaging immediately is the most appropriate response. In those situations, staying present, addressing the issue directly, and working through the discomfort is what allows growth to occur. There will also be times where immediate engagement is not the best option, and delaying the response becomes the more effective choice. What matters is not which of those paths you take in a given moment, but whether your response leads back to engagement.

This is something Alex continued to work through as he developed more consistency. There were situations where he learned to stay engaged and respond in the moment, particularly as he became more comfortable with direct communication. There were also situations where he recognized that he was not in the right position to respond effectively and needed to wait until he could approach the situation with more clarity. The difference was that he was no longer stepping away without returning. Whether he engaged immediately or delayed intentionally, the situation was eventually addressed.

As this process continues, the pattern becomes more stable. The decisions you make begin to align more consistently with your intention to grow. Situations that once triggered automatic avoidance become opportunities to choose a different response. Over time, this consistency improves your ability to become more effective and that is a key to overcoming anxiety, depression and suicidal thoughts.

It is also important to again emphasize that this process will not be perfect. There will still be moments where you avoid something that should have been addressed, or where you delay without following through. Those moments are part of the process, not evidence that change is not working. What matters is your ability to recognize them and return to engagement rather than allowing them to become the dominant pattern again.

The distinction between avoidance and delay is not something you apply once and then move past. It becomes an ongoing part of how you respond to challenges over time. Each time you engage intentionally, you reinforce a pattern that builds capacity and resilience. Each time you recognize avoidance and return to engagement, you interrupt the patterns that previously kept you stuck.

As you continue moving forward, the goal is not to eliminate discomfort or to create a life where everything is easy. The goal is to become someone who can respond to what is in front of them in a way that leads to growth. Understanding when to engage immediately and when to delay intentionally is a key part of that process, because it allows you to respond with greater clarity instead of reacting automatically to what you are experiencing.

Over time, this distinction becomes less of a conscious effort and more of a consistent pattern. You begin to recognize when something needs to be addressed, when it needs to be delayed, and how to return to it in a way that creates movement. That consistency is what allows the broader changes described in this book to take hold, because it ensures that the situations that matter are not left unresolved.

Chapter 5 Summary

- Avoidance and delay can look similar on the surface, but they function very differently depending on whether you return to engage with the situation.
- Avoidance removes the need to deal with what is difficult, while delay is an intentional decision to engage more effectively at a later time.
- Delay only functions as growth when it includes a clear commitment to reengage; without that commitment, it becomes avoidance.
- Effective delay requires identifying an appropriate time, place, and audience to address the situation rather than reacting immediately.
- Immediate reactions often feel productive, but mature responses consider whether the conditions are right for engagement and choose the most effective way to move forward.

CHAPTER 6

Where to Start

At this point, you understand the system. You know that your direction is shaped by how you respond to adversity, that confidence is built through repeated engagement, and that meaningful progress comes from confronting what is difficult rather than avoiding it. The next question becomes practical: where do you actually begin, especially when it feels like there are multiple areas of your life that need attention?

As we have alluded to, one of the most common mistakes people make at this stage is trying to fix everything at once. When you see clearly how many areas of your life could improve, it is natural to feel a sense of urgency and want to take action in all of them simultaneously. The problem is that this approach almost always leads to overwhelm, and overwhelm often leads right back into avoidance. Instead of making progress, people become discouraged and stop before anything meaningful has changed.

The starting point is much simpler than that. You begin by choosing one life area and identifying one meaningful place to engage within it. That does not mean you are ignoring the rest of your life. It means you are choosing a starting point that allows you to create real, measurable progress without overwhelming yourself.

To do that effectively, you first need to define what success would look like in that area. This is not about creating a perfect or idealized version of your life. It is about identifying a direction that reflects the kind of person you want to become and the kind of life you want to build. Once that vision is clear enough to guide you, you can begin to define goals and the steps required to move toward it.

At this point, it is important to be precise about what a goal actually is, because many people use the word loosely. A meaningful goal is not just a general intention or a hope that things will improve. A useful way to define a goal is through a simple framework. It should involve a **specific behavior**, something that you can clearly identify. It should be **measurable**, so you can determine whether you actually did it. It should be **achievable**, meaning it is realistic given your current situation. It should be **relevant**, so it directly connects to the vision you are trying to move toward. And it should be **time-bound**, so there is a clear point at which you can evaluate whether you followed through. When these elements are present, a goal becomes something you can act on rather than something you simply think about.

Once you have identified a meaningful goal, the next step is to break those steps down into smaller, actionable parts. This is where many people get stuck, because they keep their goals too large and abstract. A helpful way to approach this is to break your goals into what you might think of as bite-sized chunks. These are small actions that can be completed in a short amount of time, ideally in about **fifteen minutes or less**. This approach allows you to take something that feels overwhelming and turn it into multiple small mini-steps that are immediately actionable.

When you break a larger goal into these smaller pieces, you give yourself a clear starting point for each day and create opportunities to make progress whenever you find an extra fifteen minutes in your schedule. Instead of wondering where to begin, you can simply look at your list and choose one action that moves you forward. If you have more time or energy, you can complete additional steps, but even a single fifteen-minute effort is enough to create real progress. Over time, these small actions accumulate and lead to meaningful results.

It is also important to make this process tangible. Writing your goals and your daily actions down on paper, rather than simply thinking about them or typing them into a device, has been shown to improve memory, engagement, and follow-through. The act of writing engages more of your brain and makes the information more concrete, which increases the likelihood that you will act on it.

There is an additional benefit to this approach. When you complete an action, you can physically mark it off, whether that means crossing it out or checking it off your list. That simple act creates a sense of completion and reinforces the behavior. Over time, this builds a positive feedback loop where taking action and completing tasks becomes increasingly rewarding, which increases the likelihood that you will continue.

As you take these steps, it is important to expect some discomfort. If the goal is meaningful, it will require you to engage with something that is unfamiliar, uncertain, or difficult. That discomfort is not a sign that you are doing something wrong. It is often a sign that you are doing exactly what is needed for growth. When you understand that ahead of time, you are less likely to interpret discomfort as a reason to stop.

It is also important to recognize that progress will not always feel satisfying in the moment. There will be times when you take a step forward and it feels small, awkward, or even unsuccessful. In those moments, it is easy to think that what you are doing is not working. But if you look at it through the framework we have built, you can see that you are still adding to your experience. You are still building your ability to handle what is in front of you, and that process is what leads to meaningful change over time.

As you continue to take steps in that one area, something begins to happen. You start to build confidence. You begin to see that you can engage with things that once felt overwhelming. As that confidence grows, people often begin experiencing something else that had previously been missing: a deeper sense of being capable, valued, and connected to the people and goals that matter most to them.

At some point, you will reach a place where you can begin to expand your focus. You may start to identify another area of your life that needs attention, or you may recognize that progress in one area is limited by avoidance in another. When that happens, you do not abandon what you have already started. You build on it. You continue to engage in the first area while beginning to take steps in another.

This is how momentum is created. It is not the result of a single large effort. It is the result of consistent, repeated engagement over time. Each step builds on the one before it, and over time those steps begin to create a shift that is difficult to reverse.

It is also important to recognize that there will be times when you feel stuck or unsure how to move forward. In some areas, you may be able to clearly define your goals and take action without much difficulty. In others, you may encounter a mental block where it is difficult to even define what success would look like. When that happens, it is often a signal that the area involves deeper patterns, past experiences, or emotional complexity that may require support.

Seeking help in those moments is not a step backward. It is a form of confrontation. It is an acknowledgment that you are engaging with something that matters enough to require additional resources. Whether that support comes from therapy, mentorship, or another trusted source, the key is that you are still moving toward the problem rather than away from it.

As you begin this process, it is helpful to keep your focus on direction rather than perfection. You are not trying to eliminate all down arrows immediately or solve every problem at once. Over time, engaging with difficulty begins to feel more natural and consistent, and the changes you create begin to stabilize. This is how you start: by choosing one area, defining a meaningful goal, breaking it into small actionable steps, and consistently engaging with it even when it is uncomfortable.

As you do that, you begin to build confidence, create momentum, and gradually expand your ability to handle what is in front of you. The process is simple, but it is not easy. It requires effort, consistency, and a willingness to face things you would rather avoid. At the same time, it is reliable. If you continue engaging with what is meaningful over time, the direction of your life begins to change, and that is where real change begins.

Chapter 6 Summary

- Change begins by choosing one life area and consistently engaging with it rather than trying to fix everything at once.
- Meaningful goals require a clear vision of success and must be specific, measurable, achievable, relevant, and time-bound.
- Large goals become manageable when they are broken into small, actionable steps that can be completed consistently over time.
- Discomfort is a normal part of growth and should not be interpreted as a sign that you are failing or moving in the wrong direction.
- Progress builds confidence gradually, and consistent engagement in one area creates momentum that can expand into other areas of life.
- Seeking support is a form of confrontation when it helps you move toward the problem rather than avoid it.

CHAPTER 7

Building Momentum

Once you have started taking action, the next challenge is not understanding what to do. The next challenge is continuing to do it when it becomes difficult, repetitive, or initially less rewarding than you expected. Starting is important, but what determines whether your life actually changes is whether you continue long enough for that effort to compound.

In the beginning, progress often feels motivating because you see movement quickly and experience an initial sense of excitement. This early phase can create the impression that change will continue to feel energizing and rewarding. However, as you move into the middle phase of progress, the work you are doing is just as important, but the results often become less obvious, improvements feel like they have slowed down, and the initial excitement begins to fade. This is the point where many people struggle, not because the process has stopped working, but because it no longer feels the way it did at the start.

This is also where a very common pattern emerges. Instead of continuing to engage with the same goal, many people begin to shift their focus to something new. They start another project, set a different goal, or move toward something that feels more interesting or rewarding in the moment. Some people who are stuck in this cycle will describe themselves as an "idea person," believing that their strength is coming up with new concepts while others are responsible for carrying them out. While this may feel like an accurate description, the reality is that most people are capable of generating ideas. The difference between those who create meaningful change and those who remain stuck is not who has the idea, but who continues to work on it after the initial excitement fades. When people consistently move from one idea to the next without finishing what they started, it often reflects a pattern of avoidance rather than a lack of creativity.

This was something Alex struggled with repeatedly as he began making progress. Early on, each new area of growth felt exciting because it created movement and produced a sense of hope that had been missing for a long time. As he started building routines, engaging socially, and taking more responsibility, he experienced periods where the progress itself felt energizing. The problem emerged later, once those same behaviors became more familiar and required consistent repetition rather than emotional excitement.

At that stage, he began to feel discouraged because the new behaviors that had initially felt rewarding no longer produced the same emotional intensity. Instead of recognizing this as a normal part of sustained growth, his instinct was often to search for something new that would recreate the same sense of excitement. He would come into therapy talking about a completely different goal, project, or direction that suddenly felt extremely important and emotionally energizing compared to the slower, repetitive work he was already doing.

Over time, I began referring to these as "shiny objects." The issue was not that the new ideas were necessarily bad. In many cases, they were reasonable goals. The problem was the timing and function they were serving. Often, he had not yet practiced the current behaviors long enough for them to become stable, automatic, and integrated into his daily life. Moving too quickly toward a new goal at that stage risked abandoning the very habits and routines that were beginning to create meaningful change.

As we worked through this pattern, he eventually started keeping a list of these shiny objects rather than immediately acting on them. Instead of treating every new idea as something that required immediate pursuit, he learned to evaluate whether the new goal represented meaningful expansion of his current efforts or whether it was functioning as an escape from the discomfort, boredom, or repetition that naturally occur in the middle phase of growth.

This became an important turning point because it helped him recognize that sustained progress often stops feeling exciting long before it starts producing major long-term results. The emotional intensity fades first, and many people mistakenly interpret that loss of excitement as evidence that the process is no longer working. In reality, this is often the exact point where meaningful momentum is beginning to develop.

Learning to stay engaged after the novelty fades is one of the most important parts of long-term growth. It is also one of the clearest distinctions between people who repeatedly start over and people who build lasting change over time.

This pattern is especially important to recognize because it can look like a lack of focus or discipline. In some cases, people attribute this to conditions like ADHD, and while there are legitimate neurological factors that can affect attention and focus, there is also a behavioral component that is often overlooked. The ability to remain engaged when something is no longer new, fun, or emotionally stimulating is not just a function of brain capacity. It is also a skill that is developed through repeated practice of continuing to engage when motivation decreases. This capacity to continue engaging when motivation fades is what people commonly refer to as "discipline". When that skill is not developed, it can amplify difficulties with focus and consistency over time.

Momentum is built when you continue to engage even after the initial motivation fades. It is the result of consistent behavior, not emotional intensity. When you rely on temporary motivation, you are dependent on how you feel in the moment. When you rely on consistent disciplined action, you create a pattern that continues regardless of how you feel.

This is why discipline becomes so important. Discipline is not about forcing yourself to do something extreme. It is about following through on the commitments you have made to yourself, especially when you do not feel like it. It is the ability to continue taking those small, meaningful fifteen-minute steps even when they feel inconvenient, repetitive, or uncomfortable. Everyone experiences moments where motivation fades, but those who continue to move in an upward direction are the ones who choose to engage at some level anyway. Even if they cannot do everything they planned, they still take one step, complete one small action, and maintain forward movement.

This leads to an important distinction. There will be times when your energy is low or your capacity is limited, and in those moments, it may be necessary to slow down. Slowing down is not the same as stopping. When you slow down, you adjust your effort to match your current state, but you continue to move forward. When you stop completely, you move into avoidance. Maintaining even a small amount of engagement keeps the cycle moving in the right direction and prevents the loss of momentum that occurs when you disengage entirely.

As you continue to take action, it is normal to experience fluctuations in how you feel. Some days will feel productive and encouraging, while others will feel slow, frustrating, or discouraging. These fluctuations do not mean the process is failing. They are a natural part of sustained effort. The key is to continue moving forward even when progress feels less noticeable.

There will also be times when you miss a day, fall behind, or feel like you have lost progress. When that happens, it is easy to interpret it as failure and stop altogether. The more effective response is to recognize that setbacks are part of the process and to re-engage as quickly as possible. One missed step does not erase the progress you have made, but consistently avoiding re-engagement will.

As you continue to move forward, you will begin to notice that your discipline increases and the effort required to initiate action decreases over time. What once felt difficult begins to feel more routine. This is not because the work has changed, but because you have changed. You have built the experience and confidence necessary to handle it more effectively. As this process continues, people often begin to experience a deeper sense of confidence and self-respect because they are building evidence that they can continue engaging even when things become difficult, repetitive, or emotionally unrewarding.

Momentum also begins to influence how you approach new challenges. As you build confidence in one area, you are more likely to engage in others. The process becomes more familiar, and the hesitation that once held you back begins to decrease. This is how growth expands beyond a single area and starts to shape your life more broadly.

It is important to remember that momentum and discipline are not something you achieve once and then keep automatically. They are something you maintain through continued engagement. When you stop engaging, momentum slows and can eventually reverse. When you continue engaging consistently, even at a small level, momentum rebuilds and becomes easier to sustain over time.

As you continue applying this process, you will begin to see that momentum is not dependent on feeling motivated or inspired. It is the natural result of consistent action over time. What once required a significant amount of effort to initiate begins to feel more natural because you have built the experience, the tolerance for discomfort, and the confidence necessary to engage more easily with what is in front of you.

This is how progress becomes sustainable. It is not driven by bursts of energy or short periods of intensity, but by a steady pattern of engagement that continues even when the process feels less exciting than it did at the beginning. As that pattern strengthens, it becomes something you can rely on, and the direction of your life begins to stabilize in a way that no longer depends on how you feel in any given moment.

Over time, this creates a shift that is difficult to reverse. The same way that repeated avoidance leads to stagnation and increased difficulty, repeated engagement leads to growth, increased capability, and a stronger sense that you can handle what is in front of you. This does not eliminate challenges, but it changes how you respond to them, and that response is what ultimately determines the direction of your life.

Chapter 7 Summary

- Real change depends less on initial motivation and more on continuing to engage after the excitement fades.
- Many people avoid the difficult middle phase of growth by jumping to new ideas or projects instead of continuing what they started.
- Discipline is the ability to continue taking meaningful action even when motivation, excitement, or emotional reward decreases.
- Slowing down is not the same as stopping; maintaining even small amounts of engagement prevents momentum from reversing into avoidance.
- Setbacks, low-energy periods, and fluctuations in motivation are normal parts of sustained growth and do not erase previous progress.
- Consistent engagement over time builds momentum, increases confidence, and gradually makes meaningful action feel more natural and sustainable.

CHAPTER 8

When You Get Stuck

At some point in this process, you are going to feel stuck, and that is not a possibility but a certainty. No matter how clearly you understand the system or how well you begin applying it, there will be times when your progress slows down, your motivation drops, and the actions that once felt manageable begin to feel difficult again. When that happens, many people assume something has gone wrong or that they have somehow failed, but that assumption is incorrect. Getting stuck is not a sign that the process is broken. It is part of the process itself, and the question is not whether you will experience it, but how you respond when it happens.

There are several ways that feeling stuck tends to show up, and understanding them helps you respond more effectively. Sometimes it is emotional, where you know what you need to do but do not feel like doing it because the discomfort feels stronger than usual. Other times it is cognitive, where you are willing to act but are unsure what the next step should be, and the path forward feels unclear. In other cases, it is behavioral, where you were making progress but stopped due to an interruption and have not re-engaged. All of these are normal experiences, but if they are not addressed, they tend to lead to the same outcome, which is a shift into avoidance.

One of the most important things to understand is that many

people get stuck not because they lack motivation, but because they lack clarity. When you do not know exactly what to do next, your brain experiences that as uncertainty, and uncertainty often leads to overwhelm. That overwhelm makes avoidance feel like the easiest option.

This was something Alex struggled with repeatedly as he continued trying to build momentum in his life. After some of the initial excitement of making progress had worn off, he began coming into therapy describing what he called "brain fog." He explained that when he tried to think about what he needed to do next, his thoughts felt scattered and unclear. He would sit down intending to engage with a goal, but instead he would become mentally overwhelmed and drift back toward distraction, old habits, or the feeling that he simply could not think clearly enough to move forward.

As we explored this more carefully, it became clear that much of the problem was not a lack of ability, but a lack of clearly defined next steps. In some areas of life, his vision of success was still extremely shallow. He had only thought through the first step of what success might require, but not the next several layers beyond that. In other areas, he had never taken the time to learn what would actually be required to move forward at all. Because the path remained vague, his brain experienced it as overwhelming and difficult to approach.

This is where learning becomes part of confrontation. When you are stuck because you do not know what to do, seeking information is not avoidance if it is done with the intention of acting. This may involve watching a video, asking for guidance, attending therapy, reading, researching, or breaking the problem down until you understand the steps required to move forward. Once you have that clarity, you can return to the fifteen-minute rule and define a small, manageable action that allows you to re-engage. In this way, education is not a replacement for action, but a tool that makes action possible.

This became a major turning point for Alex. Initially, Alex interpreted uncertainty as proof that he could not move forward. However, as he continued engaging in therapy, he gradually began viewing it as a signal that he needed more clarity instead. Sometimes that meant researching how other people had solved similar problems. Other times, it meant discussing the problem in therapy and then sitting down to build additional SMART goals that broke larger responsibilities into smaller, more actionable parts. Once those steps became clearer, the "brain fog" often decreased significantly because the next action no longer felt abstract or undefined. Eventually, he developed the ability to perform this process even without a therapist's assistance.

Another major factor in getting stuck is the environment you are operating in. In many cases, people expect themselves to succeed in environments that are set up for failure. If your surroundings make avoidance easier than engagement, you will constantly be working against yourself. A simple example of this is dieting. If someone is trying to change their eating habits but keeps their environment filled with the foods they are trying to avoid, they are creating a situation where failure is the most accessible option. The same principle applies to many areas of life. When possible, adjusting your environment so that the easier choice is the one that supports your goals can significantly increase your ability to stay engaged.

This was another area where Alex began to make meaningful changes. As he became more aware of his patterns, he started noticing how aspects of his environment were reinforcing avoidance and dependency. One important example involved his living situation with his grandmother. For years, many basic responsibilities had been handled for him automatically. Meals were often prepared for him, decisions were made for him, and many opportunities for independent engagement had quietly been removed.

At one point, he took this lesson learned in therapy and applied it. He sat down with his grandmother and explained that he felt he needed to start taking on more responsibility himself, even if it meant doing things imperfectly at first. He specifically told her that she did not always need to cook dinner for him and that he needed to begin learning how to handle more of those responsibilities on his own. His grandmother graciously agreed and together they started creating an environment where he would take on these new tasks. He understood that he didn't yet have the cooking and cleaning skills but also realized that he would never develop them while grandma did those things for him. His suspicions proved accurate as some initial meals and cleaning attempts went poorly at first and mistakes happened. But by facing these new challenges, he learned the basics of cooking and cleaning and his confidence started growing.

This was an important moment because it represented a shift from simply understanding the concepts intellectually to actively restructuring his environment in a way that supported engagement instead of avoidance. Rather than waiting until he felt fully confident or prepared, he began practicing those responsibilities directly. While there were a few meals that didn't turn out, online videos eventually proved effective and he started to become an adequate cook. But even more importantly, he was learning age-appropriate independence and gaining confidence in his ability to function more independently as an adult.

It is also important to recognize that feeling stuck often triggers a shift in how people think about themselves. Instead of seeing it as a temporary state, they begin interpreting it as evidence that they are incapable of change. They may feel like they have lost all of their progress or that they are back at the beginning. In reality, that is not what is happening. The experience, confidence, and skills you have built do not disappear simply because you paused. What matters is what you do next, because if you respond by disengaging further, you reinforce avoidance, and if you respond by taking even a small step forward, you reinforce engagement.

There are also cases where the ability to get unstuck was never fully developed in the first place. Some individuals grow up in environments where others consistently removed difficulty for them, stepped in to solve problems, or prevented them from experiencing discomfort. While the intention may have been protective, the result is that the individual does not develop the ability to persist through difficulty on their own. When those individuals later face challenges without that support, they may feel stuck more quickly, have a harder time re-engaging, and experience significantly more anxiety, discouragement, depression, or suicidal thoughts as a result. This is not a permanent limitation, but it does mean that learning how to persist becomes an important part of their growth moving forward.

The most important skill in this entire process is not avoiding getting stuck, but learning how to re-engage when you do. When you feel stuck, the goal is not to solve everything at once, but to move again. That movement may be small, and it may not feel significant, but it is enough to shift your direction. Returning to a single, clearly defined step and taking action on it is what brings you back into the process.

Over time, the ability to get unstuck becomes one of the most valuable skills you can develop. It is not about maintaining perfect consistency or avoiding difficulty. It is about recognizing when you have slowed down or stopped and choosing to move forward again. That decision, repeated over time, is what keeps the Adversity Cycle moving in an upward direction and allows progress to continue even when the process becomes difficult.

Chapter 8 Summary

- Getting stuck is not a failure; it is a normal and expected part of the change process.
- Many people get stuck not because they lack motivation, but because they lack clarity about the next meaningful step.
- Seeking information, guidance, or education is a form of confrontation when it is used to support action rather than replace it.
- Your environment strongly influences whether engagement or avoidance becomes the easier choice.
- Learning to re-engage after feeling stuck is one of the most important skills in long-term growth and change.
- Small, clearly defined actions are often enough to restore momentum and keep the Adversity Cycle moving upward.

CHAPTER 9

Your Past Still Influences You

Up to this point, we have focused on what you can do moving forward. You have learned how the Adversity Cycle works, how confidence is built, how avoidance shows up, and how to begin taking action even when it feels difficult. All of that is essential, because it gives you a way to change the direction of your life starting now. At the same time, it is important to understand that the patterns you are working to change did not develop randomly, and they are not occurring in isolation from your past.

Your past has shaped how you respond to adversity, and much of that influence happens at a level that is not fully conscious. The way you think, the way you interpret discomfort, and the way you respond to stress have often been practiced so many times that they become automatic. In psychology and neuroscience, this is sometimes referred to as habituation, which means that you are engaging in patterns of behavior without needing to consciously think through each step. This is similar to how someone can drive a familiar route and realize they arrived without actively thinking through every turn, because the behavior has been learned and automated over time.

In the same way, many of your emotional and behavioral responses are driven by patterns that were developed earlier in life and are now being carried out automatically. This does not mean you are stuck with them, but it does mean that they will continue to operate until they are intentionally retrained. That retraining process takes time and repeated effort, and while we will touch on it here, a more detailed explanation of how to retrain those patterns is discussed in my earlier work on trauma and recovery.

This does not mean that your past determines your future, but it does mean that it influences your starting point. Some people begin with patterns that make it easier to engage with adversity, while others begin with patterns that make avoidance more likely. Over time, these differences can influence how often someone experiences anxiety, how intense that anxiety feels, and how they respond when faced with challenges. The same is true for depression, where patterns of withdrawal and avoidance can become more deeply reinforced when they are practiced repeatedly over time.

Many of these patterns are shaped by early environments. Some individuals are encouraged to take on challenges, experience failure, and learn how to recover and adapt. Others are raised in environments where discomfort is minimized, where challenges are removed, or where stepping outside of a defined role is discouraged. In those situations, the intention is often to protect, but the long-term effect can be that the individual has fewer opportunities to build the life skills needed to handle adversity. Over time, this can contribute to patterns of avoidance that make anxiety, depression, and even suicidal thinking more likely to persist or intensify.

It is important to recognize that these patterns often developed for a reason. Avoiding conflict may have helped maintain stability in a difficult environment. Staying quiet may have prevented situations from escalating. Focusing on what felt safe may have been the best available option at the time. In that context, those responses were adaptive. The challenge is that patterns that were once helpful can become limiting when your environment changes and you are no longer in the same circumstances that required those responses.

Understanding this creates an important shift. It allows you to see your behavior not as a fixed part of who you are, but as a learned pattern that can be changed. At the same time, it is important to approach this with accuracy rather than blame. There is value in understanding how previous experiences shaped your current responses, because recognizing those patterns is often the first step toward changing them. Many people cannot begin improving until they first acknowledge the reality of what has been happening in their life and how those patterns developed over time.

At the same time, understanding how you got here is only the beginning of the process. If a person or therapist remains permanently focused on explaining current struggles only through past experiences, then growth eventually stops and the focus itself can become another form of avoidance. At some point, responsibility has to shift toward how a person chooses to respond in the present. While past experiences may explain many of the patterns that developed, they do not permanently remove a person's ability to engage differently moving forward.

When this shift does not happen, people often begin viewing themselves and the world in an increasingly all-or-nothing way. Life becomes divided into categories of damaged or healthy, broken or successful, hopeless or fixed. This type of black-and-white thinking leaves very little room for gradual growth, adaptation, accountability, or meaningful change over time.

This was something Alex struggled with deeply at one point in the process. As he became more aware of how much he had avoided throughout his life and how underdeveloped many areas of his life still felt, he began to interpret those realizations in an extremely black-and-white way. He initially described himself as a helpless victim because his parents had abandoned him and his grandmother did too much for him. He described it as if his future had already been decided. He explained that he felt too far gone, that he would always be seen as incompetent, and that because he had not started from a strong place, he would never become someone capable, respected, or desirable as a future partner.

In his mind, people were divided into two categories. Some people seemed to start life from a good place and naturally become successful, confident, and capable, while others, like him, started from a broken place and would never truly recover. Because he had struggled socially, emotionally, and professionally for so long, he believed his failures permanently defined him. If he had not been "good enough" from the beginning, then he assumed there was no room to grow and he never could become good later.

What he could not yet see at first was that nearly everything we had discussed throughout this book depended on the opposite assumption. The entire Adversity Cycle is based on the idea that people change through repeated engagement over time. Confidence is built. Self-esteem is built. Emotional stability is built. These things are not fixed traits that are permanently assigned at the beginning of life. They develop gradually through repeated up arrows, repeated confrontation, repeated learning, and repeated engagement with adversity over time.

Over time, however, he slowly began recognizing that his future was not as hopeless as he had originally believed. But this did not shift quickly for him. Even after he intellectually understood the concept, the emotional patterns connected to his past continued influencing how he saw himself. There were still moments where discouragement, shame, anxiety, depression, and hopelessness would pull him back toward the belief that he was permanently damaged and would always be behind everyone else. At times, he still struggled with thoughts that his future would never improve enough for his life to feel meaningful or stable. The difference was that he gradually stopped allowing those thoughts to completely determine his direction.

This process took years, not weeks. It was built through repeated up arrows, repeated engagement, repeated setbacks, and repeated decisions to continue anyway. At the same time, something important began happening long before he fully reached the goals he was working toward. His mood began improving as he started making progress and his outlook of what was possible became more realistic. His anxiety slowly became more manageable, and over time his suicidal thoughts became less frequent and eventually stopped occurring altogether.

What mattered was not that he had already achieved everything he wanted. What mattered was that his life had begun moving in a different direction. The hopelessness he once felt started to weaken as he accumulated more experiences of confronting difficulty, making progress, and realizing that his future was not fixed in the way he once believed.

The improvements were small at first. There were still setbacks, difficult days, and moments where old patterns resurfaced. However, as he continued engaging consistently over time, the progress became more stable. His past still influenced him, but it was no longer the only thing shaping how he viewed himself. As he continued building confidence, developing relationships, and taking on more responsibility, his future and the possibility of who he was becoming began to influence him as well. Eventually, that future-oriented perspective became stronger than the assumptions that had previously defined him.

Over time, the same person who once believed he would never be capable of meaningful relationships or independent adult functioning eventually developed the ability to sustain both. He eventually entered a healthy romantic relationship, married, and developed the ability to maintain work that allowed him to support a family. As his perspective changed, the way he interpreted the people around him began to change as well. He was able to see his grandmother's sacrifices and appreciate that while not perfect, she was doing the best she could and their relationship developed into a beautiful age-appropriate connection. The important point is not that his past disappeared. It is that his future gradually began exerting a stronger influence on his life than his past did.

This is where responsibility becomes important, and it needs to be understood in the right way. There is a difference between recognizing that your past influenced you and believing that it removes your ability to act in the present. When you were younger and dependent on others, there were many things you could not control, and the environment around you played a major role in shaping your experiences. As you become more independent, however, your ability to influence your own life increases, and with that increased ability comes increased responsibility.

This does not mean you are expected to ignore your past or pretend it did not affect you. It means that you are no longer limited to responding the way you once had to. You now have the ability to evaluate those patterns and decide whether you want to continue them or change them. Taking responsibility in this context is not about blame. It is about recognizing that you have the ability to influence what happens next, regardless of where you started.

There are also situations where the patterns you are trying to change are more complex and more difficult to work through on your own. In those cases, seeking support can be an important part of the process. This does not mean something is wrong with you. It means you are working through patterns that developed over time and may require additional perspective or guidance to fully understand and change. Choosing to seek that kind of support is not avoidance. It is a form of confrontation, because you are actively engaging with something that matters rather than moving away from it.

As you continue applying what you have learned, you will begin to see how your past and your present interact. You will notice situations where your initial response is driven by an old pattern, and you will have the opportunity to choose a different response. Those moments are where real change happens, because each time you choose to respond differently, you begin retraining those automatic patterns.

Over time, those new responses begin replacing the old ones. The patterns that once limited you start to lose their influence, and your ability to engage with your life in a more effective way continues to grow. This does not erase your past, but it changes the role it plays in your life and how much influence it has over your future.

Chapter 9 Summary

- Your past influences how you respond to adversity, but it does not permanently determine your future.
- Many emotional and behavioral responses operate automatically because they were learned and reinforced repeatedly over time.
- Patterns that were once adaptive or protective can later become limiting when your environment and responsibilities change.
- Progress and emotional improvement often begin long before major life goals are fully achieved.
- Responsibility is not about blaming yourself for your past; it is about recognizing your ability to influence what happens next.
- Lasting change occurs through repeated engagement over time, where new patterns gradually begin to exert a stronger influence on your life than old ones.

CHAPTER 10

Your Future Begins Now

When Alex first came to therapy, he did not believe his future could meaningfully improve. At the time, his anxiety was overwhelming, his depression was severe, he regularly experienced thoughts that life would never truly get better and he regularly experienced suicidal thoughts. He struggled socially, had very little confidence, and did not know how to function independently in many areas of life. Most of his time was spent avoiding discomfort and retreating into activities that felt safe, familiar, and predictable. He wanted relief from anxiety, depression, and suicidal thoughts, but he did not yet understand that improvement would only become possible when he started responding differently to adversity.

Initially, even very small forms of engagement felt overwhelming. Conversations were difficult. Responsibilities felt exhausting. Situations that most people would consider ordinary often felt impossible to navigate. Much of his life was organized around avoiding discomfort rather than confronting it, and because of that, his world had gradually become smaller and more restricted over time.

What made this especially painful was that he initially believed these struggles permanently defined him. He did not see himself as someone who was behind and capable of improving. He saw himself as someone fundamentally flawed who would always remain that way. Because he had not started from a strong place socially, emotionally, or professionally, he believed he would never become competent, successful, or capable of building a meaningful future. In his mind, people either started strong or they stayed broken. There was no opportunity for change or growth.

That way of thinking was a form of avoidance that kept him trapped for a long time because it left no room for gradual growth. If improvement had to happen immediately or perfectly, then every mistake became evidence that nothing would ever change. What he could not yet see was that meaningful change rarely happens all at once. It happens through repeated up arrows over time, often in ways that feel small or insignificant in the moment. But there was hope because he was willing to engage with the process instead of continuing to avoid it.

The middle phase of his growth was messy, uncomfortable, and inconsistent. He began learning how to stay engaged in difficult conversations instead of avoiding them. He started recognizing when discomfort was triggering down arrows and gradually practiced responding differently. He learned how to tolerate hurt without automatically interpreting it as harm. He struggled through awkward social situations, misunderstood people, became discouraged, got stuck, and repeatedly had to re-engage after setbacks.

There were times where progress felt exciting and motivating, and there were other times where the novelty wore off and the process felt repetitive and emotionally unrewarding. During those periods, he often became distracted by what we eventually referred to as "shiny objects," new goals, ideas, or directions that felt more exciting than the slower work of continuing to build the habits and skills he had already started developing. Over time, he learned to recognize that pattern and realized that meaningful growth often stops feeling exciting long before it starts producing major long-term results.

There were also periods where he felt mentally overwhelmed and struggled with what he described as "brain fog." At times, he wanted to engage but genuinely did not know what the next step should be. In some areas, his vision of success was so underdeveloped that he had never clearly thought through what would actually be required to move forward. Instead of interpreting that confusion as proof that he was incapable, he gradually learned how to seek clarity, break problems into smaller steps, and continue engaging even when he felt uncertain.

As this process continued, something important began happening long before he fully reached the goals he wanted. **He started improving as he made progress.** His anxiety became more manageable. His depression lightened. The hopelessness that once dominated his thinking slowly began to weaken. Over time, his suicidal thoughts became less frequent and eventually stopped occurring altogether. What changed first was not that his life suddenly became perfect, but that his direction changed.

This is one of the most important things to understand about growth. You do not have to wait until you have completely solved your problems before emotional relief begins to occur. As people begin confronting adversity, building confidence, creating meaningful accomplishment, and engaging more consistently with life, they often start experiencing improvements long before they fully arrive at the destination they are working toward.

The improvements are usually gradual at first. Small increases in confidence begin to accumulate. Anxiety starts becoming more manageable because situations no longer feel impossible. Depression often begins to lessen because life no longer feels completely stagnant or hopeless. As progress continues, people frequently begin experiencing something else that had previously been missing: a growing sense that their future may actually contain possibility.

This is where the balance between the past and the future begins to shift. Earlier in the process, Alex's past experiences heavily shaped how he viewed himself. His failures, avoidance, insecurity, and discouragement heavily shaped how he viewed the future. As he continued engaging over time, however, the future and the possibility of who he was becoming gradually began exerting a stronger influence on him than his past did.

That process took years, not weeks. It was built through repeated up arrows, repeated engagement, repeated setbacks, and repeated decisions to continue anyway. It involved learning how to tolerate discomfort, how to maintain momentum after the excitement faded, how to re-engage after getting stuck, and how to keep moving forward even when progress felt slow.

Over time, the changes became increasingly visible. The same person who once believed he would never be capable of meaningful relationships or independent adult functioning eventually developed both. He entered a healthy romantic relationship, eventually married, and continued learning how to share responsibility, communicate expectations, and grow alongside another person rather than avoiding discomfort within relationships. Professionally, he developed enough confidence, discipline, and consistency to sustain meaningful employment and eventually entered an electrician apprenticeship that gave him a genuine sense of accomplishment, purpose, and direction.

What makes this story important is not that his life became perfect. It is that his direction fundamentally changed. He did not eliminate every struggle, and he did not stop being influenced by his past entirely. There were still moments where insecurity, discouragement, or old patterns resurfaced. The difference was that those patterns no longer completely controlled the direction of his life.

That is the real purpose of everything discussed throughout this book. The goal is not perfection. The goal is not to become someone who never struggles, never feels anxious, or never experiences discouragement again. The goal is to become someone who consistently moves toward what matters instead of away from it.

Over time, repeatedly up arrowing begins to shape an improved identity, your confidence grows, your relationships progress, your opportunities increase, and your future becomes brighter. The same way repeated down arrows gradually move life toward increasing limitation, repeated up arrows are the key to moving your life toward increasing capability, connection, meaning, and stability.

Your past still matters. It influenced how you learned to respond to adversity, how you view yourself, and what patterns became automatic over time. At the same time, your future is not fixed by where you started. Every time you choose to engage differently, you begin influencing the direction your life moves next. Those choices may feel small in the moment, but over time they accumulate into something much larger.

This is why the Adversity Cycle matters so much. Every day, through many small decisions, you are either reinforcing the patterns that keep you stuck or building the patterns that allow growth to occur. What changes your life is not a single breakthrough moment, but the accumulation of repeated engagement over time.

You do not need to become perfect before your life improves. You do not need to erase your past before your future becomes meaningful. You simply need to begin moving consistently in a different direction and continue long enough for that direction to compound.

If you are struggling with significant anxiety, depression, hopelessness, or even suicidal thoughts, it is important to stop looking for something entirely outside of yourself to permanently solve those problems for you. While support, treatment, medication, therapy, and guidance can all play meaningful roles, none of them replace the importance of the direction your life is moving. At some point, you must honestly examine whether your daily patterns are primarily made up of up arrows or down arrows.

If your life is dominated by avoidance, disengagement, hopelessness, and movement away from what matters, then your emotional suffering will often continue regardless of how badly you want relief. The opposite is also true. As people begin repeatedly confronting adversity, engaging more consistently with life, building confidence, developing meaningful accomplishment, and creating healthier relationships, emotional improvement often begins to occur long before life becomes perfect.

This does not mean the process is fast or easy, and it does not mean there are never biological, psychological, or environmental factors involved. It means that direction matters. Repeated up arrows gradually move people toward increased capability, confidence, stability, meaning, and hope, while repeated down arrows gradually move life toward increasing limitation, discouragement, anxiety, depression, and hopelessness over time.

That is how confidence is built. That is how self-esteem develops. That is how anxiety, depression, hopelessness, and avoidance gradually begin losing their influence. And that is how people slowly become capable of building lives that once felt impossible to imagine.

Your future does not begin once everything is fixed. Your future begins now, in the small decisions you make each day about whether you are willing to continue moving toward what matters.

REFERENCES

1. Allison, K. L., & Rossouw, P. J. (2013). The therapeutic alliance: Exploring the concept of "safety" from a neuropsychotherapeutic perspective. *International Journal of Neuropsychotherapy, 1*.

2. American Psychiatric Association. (2013). *Diagnostic and statistical manual of mental disorders* (5th ed.).

3. Anelli, M., Colussi, T., et al. (2023). Rule breaking, honesty, and migration. *The Journal of Law and Economics, 66*(2).

4. Bredehoft, D. J. (2006). *Becoming a parent after growing up overindulged executive summary: Study 3*.

5. Bredehoft, D. J., Clarke, J. I., & Dawson, C. (2002). *Overindulged indicators of overindulgence scale*. http://overindulgence.org/about-our-research/our-research-scales.html

6. Bredehoft, D. J., Dawson, C., & Clarke, J. I. (2003). Relationships between childhood overindulgence, family cohesion and adaptability, self-esteem, dysfunctional attitudes, and locus of control in parents.

7. Bredehoft, D. J., Mennicke, S. A., Potter, A. M., & Clarke, J. I. (1998). Perceptions attributed by adults to parental overindulgence during childhood. *Journal of Marriage and Family Consumer Sciences Education, 16*, 3–17.

8. Campis, L., Lyman, R. D., & Prentice-Dunn, S. (1986). The parental locus of control scale: Development and validation. *Journal of Clinical Child Psychology, 15*(3), 260–

267.

9. Clarke, J. I., Dawson, C., & Bredehoft, D. J. (2014). *How much is too much? Raising likeable, responsible, respectful children—from toddlers to teens—in an age of overindulgence.* Da Capo Lifelong Press.

10. Csikszentmihalyi, M. (1990). Flow: The psychology of optimal experience. Harper & Row

11. Freed, R. D., & Tompson, M. C. (2011). Predictors of parental locus of control in mothers of pre- and early adolescents. *Journal of Clinical Child & Adolescent Psychology, 40*(1), 100–110. https://doi.org/10.1080/15374416.2011.533410

12. Freud, S. (1995). *Five lectures on psycho-analysis.* Penguin.

13. Freud, S., & Breuer, J. (1891). *Introduction to studies on hysteria.*

14. Fried, E. I., & Nesse, R. M. (2015). Depression is not a consistent syndrome: An investigation of unique symptom patterns in the STAR*D study. *Journal of Affective Disorders, 172*, 96–102. https://doi.org/10.1016/j.jad.2014.10.010

15. Harvard Health Publishing. (2022, January 10). *What causes depression?* https://www.health.harvard.edu/mind-and-mood/what-causes-depression

16. Kaufman, D. M., & Milstein, M. J. (2015). Traumatic brain injury. In *Kaufman's Clinical Neurology for Psychiatrists* (7th ed., pp. 527–536). Saunders Elsevier.

17. Lieberman, M. D. (2013). *Social: Why our brains are wired to connect.* Crown Publishers.

18. Lindkvist, R.-M., Landgren, K., et al. (2019). Predictable, collaborative and safe: Healthcare provider experiences of introducing brief admissions by self-referral for self-harming and suicidal persons with a history of extensive psychiatric inpatient care. *Issues in Mental Health Nursing, 40*(7), 548–556. https://

doi.org/10.1080/01612840.2019.1585497

19. Malcolm, J. (1998). *Psychoanalysis: The impossible profession*. Knopf Doubleday.
20. Minuchin, S., Rosman, B., et al. (1978). *Psychosomatic families*. Harvard University Press.
21. Platini, U. (2023). Study: Honest people tend to migrate toward honest areas, depriving their places of origin of human capital. *Bocconi University*. https://phys.org/news/2023-09-honest-people-tend-migrate-areas.html
22. Psychology Today. (2023). External locus of control linked to childhood overindulgence. https://www.psychologytoday.com/us/blog/the-age-of-overindulgence/202309/external-locus-of-control-linked-to-childhood-overindulgence
23. Rotter, J. B. (1954). *Social learning and clinical psychology*. Prentice-Hall. https://doi.org/10.1037/10788-000
24. Rotter, J. B. (1966). Generalized expectancies for internal versus external control of reinforcement. *Psychological Monographs, 80*(1), 1–28. https://doi.org/10.1037/h0092976
25. Sadock, B. J., Sadock, V. A., & Ruiz, P. (2015). Neural sciences. In *Kaplan & Sadock's Synopsis of Psychiatry* (11th ed.). Wolters Kluwer.
26. Sadock, B. J., Sadock, V. A., & Ruiz, P. (2015). Trauma and stressor related disorders. In *Kaplan & Sadock's Synopsis of Psychiatry* (11th ed.). Wolters Kluwer.
27. Tasman, A., Kay, J., Lieberman, J. A., First, M. B., & Maj, M. (2008). Neurobiology of anxiety disorders. In *Psychiatry* (3rd ed.). Wiley-Blackwell.
28. Welton, R., & Kay, J. (2015). The neurobiology of psychotherapy. *Psychiatric Times*. http://www.psychiatrictimes.com/neurobiology-

psychotherapy

29. Zhang, F. F., Peng, W., et al. (2018). Brain structure alterations in depression: Psychoradiological evidence. *CNS Neuroscience & Therapeutics, 24*(11), 994–1003. https://doi.org/10.1111/cns.12835

30. Abramson, L. Y., Alloy, L. B., Hogan, M. E., Whitehouse, W. G., Cornette, M., Akhavan, S., & Chiara, A. (1998). Suicidality and cognitive vulnerability to depression among college students: A prospective study. *Journal of Adolescence, 21*(2), 157–171.

31. Abramson, L. Y., Alloy, L. B., Hogan, M. E., et al. (2002). The hopelessness theory of suicidality. In *Suicide Science* (pp. xx–xx). Springer. https://doi.org/10.1007/0-306-47233-3_3

32. Angelakis, I., & Gooding, P. (2021). Experiential avoidance in non-suicidal self-injury and suicide experiences: A systematic review and meta-analysis. *Suicide and Life-Threatening Behavior, 51*(5), 978–992. https://doi.org/10.1111/sltb.12784

33. Benatov, J., Brunstein Klomek, A., et al. (2020). Doing nothing is sometimes worse: Comparing avoidant versus approach coping strategies with peer victimization and their association to depression and suicide ideation. *Journal of School Violence, 19*(4), 456–469. https://doi.org/10.1080/15388220.2020.1738941

34. Choi, H. Y., Kim, S. I., et al. (2011). A study on correlation between anxiety symptoms and suicidal ideation. *Psychiatry Investigation, 8*(4), 320–326. https://doi.org/10.4306/pi.2011.8.4.320

35. Fornaro, M., Anastasia, A., et al. (2019). The FDA "Black Box" warning on antidepressant suicide risk in young adults: More harm than benefits? *Frontiers in Psychiatry, 10*, 294. https://doi.org/10.3389/fpsyt.2019.00294

36. Friedman, R. A. (2014). Antidepressants' black-box warning — 10 years later. *New England Journal of*

Medicine, 371, 1666–1668. https://doi.org/10.1056/NEJMp1408480

37. Fu, X.-L., Li, X., et al. (2022). Blood hormones and suicidal behaviour: A systematic review and meta-analysis. *Neuroscience & Biobehavioral Reviews, 139*, 104725. https://doi.org/10.1016/j.neubiorev.2022.104725
38. Goodwin, R. D., & Roy-Byrne, P. (2006). Panic and suicidal ideation and suicide attempts: Results from the National Comorbidity Survey. *Depression and Anxiety, 23*(3), 124–132.
39. Jobes, D. A. (2023). *Managing suicidal risk: A collaborative approach* (3rd ed.). Guilford Press.
40. Martínez-Aguayo, J. C., Arancibia, M., et al. (2016). Ten years after the FDA black box warning for antidepressant drugs: A critical narrative review. *Archives of Clinical Psychiatry, 43*(3), 60–66.
41. Nam, I. (2016). Suicide bereavement and complicated grief: Experiential avoidance as a mediating mechanism. *Journal of Loss and Trauma, 21*(4), 325–334. https://doi.org/10.1080/15325024.2015.1067099
42. Nock, M. K., Borges, G., Bromet, E. J., et al. (2008). Cross-national prevalence and risk factors for suicidal ideation, plans and attempts. *British Journal of Psychiatry, 192*(2), 98–105.
43. Pagès, F., Arvers, P., Hassler, C., et al. (2004). What are the characteristics of adolescent hospitalized suicide attempters? *European Child & Adolescent Psychiatry, 13*, 151–158. https://doi.org/10.1007/s00787-004-0375-1
44. Phillips, D. P., & Ruth, T. E. (1993). Adequacy of official suicide statistics for scientific research and public policy. *Suicide and Life-Threatening Behavior, 23*, 307–319.
45. Pompili, M., Gibiino, S., et al. (2012). Prolactin and

thyroid hormone levels are associated with suicide attempts in psychiatric patients. *Psychiatry Research, 200*(2–3), 389–394. https://doi.org/10.1016/j.psychres.2012.05.010

46. Rudd, M. D. (1989). The prevalence of suicidal ideation among college students. *Suicide and Life-Threatening Behavior, 19*, 173–183. https://doi.org/10.1111/j.1943-278X.1989.tb01031.x
47. Schmideberg, M. (1936). A note on suicide. *The International Journal of Psycho-Analysis, 17*.
48. Sommer, B. (1984). *The troubled teen: Suicide, drug use, and running away*. Routledge.
49. Taliaferro, L. A., & Muehlenkamp, J. J. (2014). Risk and protective factors that distinguish adolescents who attempt suicide from those who only consider suicide in the past year. *Suicide and Life-Threatening Behavior, 44*(1), 6–22. https://doi.org/10.1111/sltb.12046
50. Wagner, B. M., Cole, R. E., & Schwartzman, P. (1995). Psychosocial correlates of suicide attempts among junior and senior high school youth. *Suicide and Life-Threatening Behavior, 25*, 358–372. https://doi.org/10.1111/j.1943-278X.1995.tb00958.x

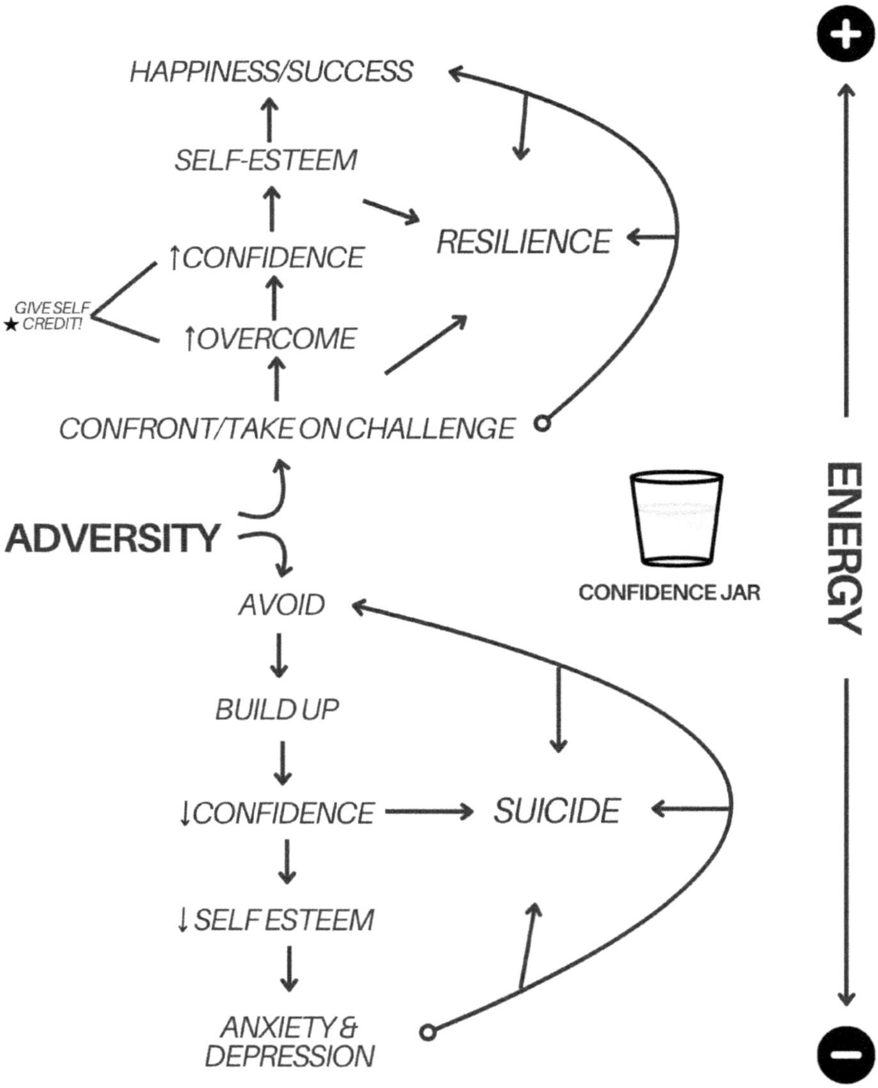
HAPPINESS/SUCCESS
SELF-ESTEEM
RESILIENCE
↑CONFIDENCE
GIVE SELF
★ CREDIT!
↑OVERCOME
CONFRONT/TAKE ON CHALLENGE
ADVERSITY
CONFIDENCE JAR
ENERGY
AVOID
BUILD UP
↓CONFIDENCE
SUICIDE
↓ SELF ESTEEM
ANXIETY &
DEPRESSION

5 LIFE AREAS

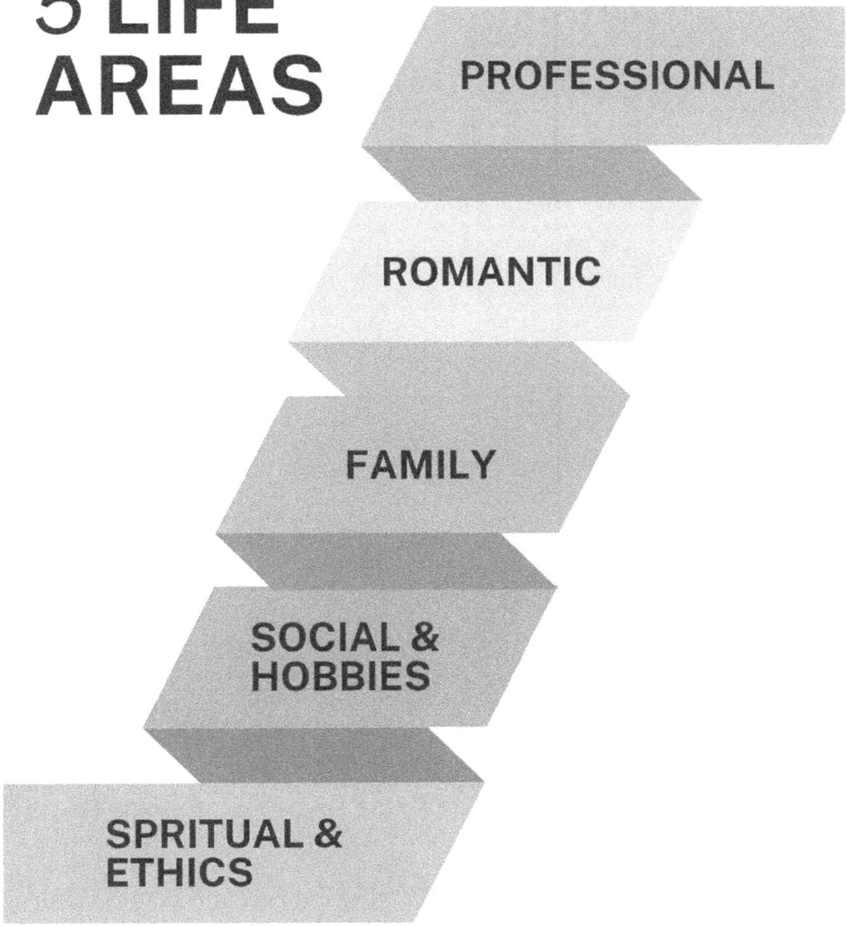
PROFESSIONAL
ROMANTIC
FAMILY
SOCIAL & HOBBIES
SPRITUAL & ETHICS

www.ingramcontent.com/pod-product-compliance
Lightning Source LLC
Chambersburg PA
CBHW050530240926
51846CB00003B/761
9781972981030